INTRODUCTION TO
GASTRONOMY

Edited by Beth Forrest and Elana Raider

**THE WORLD'S PREMIER
CULINARY COLLEGE**

University Readers™
San Diego, CA

First published in the United States of America in 2011 by University Readers, Inc.

Trademark Notice: Product or corporate names may be trademarks or registered trademarks, and are used only for identification and explanation without intent to infringe.

Cover image by Ben Fink.

15 14 13 12 11   1 2 3 4 5

Printed in the United States of America

ISBN: 978-1-60927-876-2

University Readers™
800.200.3908 I www.universityreaders.com

Contents

Identity: Are We What We Eat?   1
    By Warren Belasco

The Man Who Ate Everything   19
    By Jeffrey Steingarten

Taste   29
    By Jeremy Wolfe

Salt   61
    By Margaret Visser

Carême Dinner   67
    By Lady Morgan

The Leading Warm Sauces   69
    By Auguste Escoffier

Fernand Point's Notebook   77
    By Fernand Point and Thomas Keller

Sauces   85
    By Michel Guerard

Out of the Kitchen, Onto the Couch   99
    By Michael Pollan

The Farm-Restaurant Connection   115
    By Alice Waters

Place Matters   123
  By Amy B. Trubek

Taste in an Age of Convenience   135
  By Roger Haden

The Pleasures of Eating   151
  By Wendell Berry

IDENTITY: ARE WE WHAT WE EAT?

By Warren Belasco

> For what is food? It is not only a collection of products that can be used for statistical or nutritional studies. It is also, and at the same time, a system of communication, a body of images, a protocol of usages, situations, and behavior.
>
> Roland Barthes (1979)

We start our inquiry, to repeat Paul Rozin (1999); with the most "fundamental" and "fun" aspects of food—the way food serves to express personal and group identities and to cement social bonds. These functions may be taken for granted in our modern world, where eating is often of the "grab and go" variety and where consumers are so removed from the complex and nearly miraculous means by which solar energy and chemical elements are transformed into "dishes," "meals," and "feasts."

It is an axiom of food studies that "dining" is much more than "feeding." While all creatures "feed," only humans "dine." As the French cultural theorist Barthes suggests above, what we consider "food" extends far beyond nutrients, calories, and minerals. A meal is much more than the sum of its parts, for it encompasses what Barthes calls "a system of communication, a body of images, a protocol of usages, situations, and behavior" (Barthes 1979: 166–173). People use food to "speak" with each other, to establish rules of behavior ("protocols"), and to reveal, as Brillat-Savarin said, "what you are."

CUISINE

One way to understand the expressive and normative functions of food is through the key concept of "cuisine." In popular language the term "cuisine" is often reserved for high-class, elite, or "gourmet" food. But here, following anthropologists Peter Farb and George Armelagos (1980: 190–98), we take a more expansive view to suggest that *all* groups have an identifiable "cuisine," a shared set of "protocols," usages, communications, behaviors, etc. (A similar meaning applies to the word "culture," which extends beyond just Shakespeare, operas, and fine art to encompass a common set of ideas, images, and values that express and influence how group members think, feel, and act.) Cuisine and culture vary widely from group to group. "While the human race as a whole has tried to eat just about everything on the planet and may thus be considered to be omnivorous, specific groups are quite picky. That is, within individual cuisines certain foods are considered "good to eat" and "good to think" (yum) while others are considered "inedible" or "disgusting" (yuck).

Farb and Armelagos liken a cuisine to a culture's language—a system of communication that is inculcated from birth, if not before, and is hard to change or learn once you are grown. Even if you migrate elsewhere, you will likely retain the "accent" of your native cuisine. A similar concept is that of the "food voice," which may range, according to Annie Hauck-Lawson, from "whispers" and "utterances" to "shouts" and "choruses" (2004: 24). As with all vocalizations, some national cuisines speak more loudly than others; while Irish or Scandinavian cuisines may tend to be somewhat muted in range and resonance, Italian and Chinese are almost operatic in dramatic intensity. Similarly an individual cook's food voice may be more or less eloquent and evocative. Another way to imagine these differences in cuisine is to think in terms of menus: some restaurants (cuisines) offer long and challenging lists of complex dishes, while others stick to a short "McMenu."

Farb and Armelagos, along with culinary historian Elisabeth Rozin (1982), suggest that a group's cuisine has four main elements.

First, each cuisine prioritizes a limited set of "basic foods," the primary "edibles" selected from a broader environment of potential foods. These selections are based on a mix of convenience, identity, and responsibility considerations. As Rozin puts it, "The general rule seems to be that everyone eats some things, but no one eats all things, and the basis for the selection of foods by a culture is dependent on a wide variety of factors: availability, ease of production, nutritional costs and benefits, custom, palatability, religious or social sanction." Other analysts call these most highly prized staples "core" foods or "cultural super foods." In a seminal analysis of migrant Mexican American food practices, anthropologist Brett Williams (1984) distinguishes tortillas (the simple, daily staples) from tamales (the time-consuming dishes reserved for special occasions). "Basic foods" range from meat and potatoes in Nebraska, to stew and fufu (porridge) in West Africa, to rice and soy in East Asia, and, yes, to tortillas and beans in Central America.

Second, specific cuisines favor a distinct manner of preparing food. Rozin identifies several main "manipulative techniques," including particulation (cutting, slicing, mincing into smaller sizes), incorporation (mixing two substances to yield a third, such as the combination of water and milled grain to produce dough), marination, application of dry or wet heat, dry curing, frying, and fermentation. Such techniques vary widely depending on the energy, time, skill, personnel, and technologies available in individual kitchens. Noting how convenience and identity factors interact, Farb and Armelagos detect some "wisdom of

Box 2.1. A Holiday Meal

It is within the family that we do most of our eating. Through a complex set of domestic interactions, we learn how to eat, shop, and cook; what to like, and what to dislike. We also observe rituals, celebrate holidays, and create new traditions while discarding others. In this exercise you will apply the concept of "cuisine" to describe and interpret a festive family dinner ritual—i.e., a special meal that is planned, periodic, predictable, and especially loaded with *meaning*.

1. Introduction: What sort of meal is this and who's coming? That is, give the overall setting: type of event, time, place, personnel.
2. Food choices: Give a typical menu and tell me where the basic foods come from. Note prevailing color patterns, shapes, textures, flavor principles. Whose food preferences prevail when it comes to planning the meal? How do these foods compare with those used in daily meals?
3. Manner of preparation: Who acquires the food? Who prepares it? Describe any specialization or division of labor. Describe the main manipulative techniques. Which dishes are made "from scratch"? From a box? Where did the recipes come from? Who cleans up? Evaluate and rate the kitchen work as a theatrical performance. (Is it a good "show"?)
4. Rules for consumption: How is the meal performed? Describe:

- Time and length of meal.
- Meal site (dining room, kitchen, family room, etc.).
- Types of utensils, dishes, napkins.
- Seating arrangements at the table.
- Serving procedures.
- Aesthetic arrangement of food on the table and on the plate.
- Appropriate dress.
- Appropriate conversation topic.
- Procedures for departure from the table.
- Post-meal rituals.
- Other relevant "table manners."
- Family idiosyncrasies.
- Comparison with ordinary daily meals.

Further reading on meal rituals: Douglas 1975, Etzioni 2004, Visser 1991, Dietler and Hayden 2001, Jacobs and Scholliers 2003, Albala 2007, Pitts et al. 2007.

cuisine" in the way that some groups ingeniously exploit scarce energy resources—such as low-fat stir-frying in Asia and quick fermentation in hot and humid West Africa—but such "wisdom" is less obvious when it comes to the far less efficient microwaving of elaborately packaged "convenience foods" or the grilling of hamburgers produced in energy-intensive animal factories. Still, it is fair to say that humans have been very creative in devising numerous ways to transform the "raw" into the "cooked," and learning about such techniques is one of the delights of food studies—and a major appeal of cooking shows on television.

Cuisines are also distinguished by their "flavor principles"—a distinctive way of seasoning dishes. These unique flavoring combinations serve as important group "markers." For example, culinary identity in parts of China may be expressed through the combination of soy sauce, garlic, ginger, and sesame oil, while a mix of garlic, tomato, and olive oil may signal "southern Italian," and chili, cumin, garlic, and tomato may communicate "Mexican." To be sure, regional and personal variations in seasoning are extensive, so one must be wary of over-generalizing—except perhaps if you are a mass-marketer selling stereotypical "ethnic foods" such as tacos, spaghetti sauce, or egg rolls (Belasco 1987).

Cuisines also prescribe the way food is to be eaten—a set of "manners," codes of etiquette, Barthes's "protocols." These socially transmitted norms of behavior establish the boundaries of acceptability. As the Victorians were particularly concerned about separating the "civilized" from the "savage," their rules were particularly complex. As one 1879 rulebook put it, etiquette "is the barrier which society draws around itself, a shield against the intrusion of the impertinent, the improper, and the vulgar." But all cultures have their rules, culinary historian Margaret Visser notes, for "without them food would be hogged by the physically powerful, civility in general would decline, and eventually society would break down altogether. Furthermore the specific fashion in which a culture manages eating helps to express, identify, and dramatize that society's ideals and aesthetic style" (Visser 2003: 586, 588).

Here again notions and practices vary greatly, including the number of meals to be eaten per day, when, where, with what utensils, and with whom. Some cuisines favor pickled fish and rice for breakfast, others flaked grains with cold, pasteurized cow's milk. Some dine on the floor, others at tall tables. Some use the fingers of one hand, others use sticks, while others use prongs. Some compliment the cook with gentle burps while others finds such expressions to be unimaginably crude. In some societies women eat after men, in others at the same time but in another room.

Hierarchies of power and preference may also be expressed by the seating of guests, especially how close to the host and on which hand. Within cuisines the rules may also change depending on the importance or "weight" of a particular dining event. A casual "drink" with acquaintances entails quite a different set of protocols from a formal banquet with one's boss or in-laws. An afternoon snack may have fewer protocols than a wedding. And even weddings are celebrated with varying degrees of culinary attention. A nuptial dinner in Connecticut may take years to plan and cost a year's pay (or more), while in parts of Mali a bride may not know whom she is marrying until her wedding day, and no food at all will be served at the ensuing party (Menzel and D'Aluisio 2005: 216).

Generally, however, pleasant social gatherings involve food consumption, whereas food is usually prohibited in less friendly venues, such as traffic court, or, in keeping with the classic mind–body distinction, in many libraries and classrooms. While banning food from library stacks makes some sense, for this does protect the books, the general proscription on eating in class seems unfortunate, especially if the learning involves teamwork. According to the concept of *commensality*, sharing food has almost magical properties in its ability to turn self-seeking individuals into a collaborative group. Take, for example, the classic French folk tale, "Stone Soup." The story has many variants, but the general theme is food's transformative properties. In the midst of prolonged war, hungry soldiers stumble on a small village whose self-protective inhabitants, in standard peasant practice, have hidden all the edibles. (Potatoes in particular were especially useful for this, as they could be kept in the ground until needed.) At first the residents hesitate to share any food with the soldiers. But when the visitors state that all they need is a large stone and a pot, the peasants become curious and gather around to watch them boil the rock. Soon a soldier suggests that, while stone soup is wonderful, it would be better with a potato, and one intrigued peasant volunteers one of his own. The same happens when the cook muses about a carrot. Then meat, wine, tables, music, and so on follow. Soon the whole village is engaged in a hearty feast and the soldiers are invited to sleep in the mayor's best bed. Upon their departure the next day, the peasants send them off with many thanks, "for we shall never go hungry now that you have taught us how to make soup from stones!" (Brown 1947). The message: Sharing food makes us wiser, better people. This belief is also expressed in the Latin-based words "company" and "companions": the people with whom one shares bread.

Still, despite this general principle, an even rudimentary understanding of cultural anthropology or history suggests that many of the practices that we take to be timeless and universal are in fact highly variable and only recently "constructed." Widespread Western use of forks is relatively recent; King Louis XTV of France considered them "unmanly," while American Puritan settlers supposedly denounced them as devilish (Young 2004: 437). It was not until the mid-eighteenth century that at least half of New Englanders owned forks—and these were mostly of the "middling" classes (McWilliams 2005: 216). Many of us consider the well-mannered and elaborately equipped "family meal" to be sacrosanct, "traditional," and now endangered, yet here again we can date such rituals back only to the nineteenth century, and even then inconvenient work routines, cramped space, and limited tools kept many working families from dining together (Grover 1987, Turner 2006). Solitary eating is not a purely modern invention or affliction (Mayo 2007). Conversely, despite much moralizing to the contrary, modern families may be eating together more often than assumed, although the "rules for consumption" of a takeout *pizza* in front of the television may be quite a bit more informal and ad hoc than those idealized by Victorian gentry or depicted by Norman Rockwell.

To these four main characteristics of cuisine may be added a fifth: a distinctive infrastructure, or "food chain," by which a group's food moves from farm to fork. Some societies have very simple infrastructures—what's raised in adjacent fields is transported a short distance to a family's home, with only a few products supplied through the nearby market. Modern cuisines, on the other hand, have highly segmented and extended food chains in which a single bite may move thousands of "food miles," with many opportunities for "adding value" (profit) by countless middlemen before it finally reaches the mouth. Thus do a few cents' worth of wheat and sweeteners become a US$4 box of Frosted Flakes. The modern food supply chain includes not only the familiar farms, truckers, factories, restaurants, and supermarkets, but also research universities, government agencies (both civilian and military), agribusiness suppliers, and oil companies. If we add up all the institutions that help to feed Americans, at least twenty percent of the US workforce is involved, with an annual bill of at least US$1 trillion. Even so, despite the huge price tag, stocking the modern commissary may occupy a much smaller percentage of the population than in a society where food travels just a few steps from the back plot. Since such complex supply chains have made modern food considerably more convenient; we will examine them more closely in Chapter 4, while Chapters 5 and 6 will ponder their vast ecological, economic, and political consequences.

To illustrate these concepts, we may inquire, "What's *American* cuisine?" The question is quite complicated, as many serious scholars debate whether Americans even *have* a cuisine, or they doubt that the term is really applicable to an entity as uniquely amorphous as the USA (Mintz: 1996). Others use their answer as an opportunity to criticize "tasteless" American mass culture. When I ask undergraduate liberal arts students this question (as I do every year), I get certain predictable phrases: fast, fried, super-sized, salty, greasy, bland, and mass-marketed. Mindful of America's multicultural heritage and nature, others will cite "diversity," "the melting pot," and "creolization." Immigration historian Donna Gabaccia writes, "The American penchant to experiment with foods, to combine and mix the foods of many Cultural traditions into blended gumbos or stews, and to create 'smorgasbords' is scarcely new but is rather a recurring theme in our history as eaters" (1998: 3). Yet such celebrations of American culinary complexity are relatively recent. For a long time there *was* what might be considered a *dominant* cuisine of North America, the food beliefs and practices most associated with the heritage of British America's earliest ruling class. This hegemonic cuisine governed American cookbooks, etiquette manuals, menus, and supply chains well past the middle of the twentieth century. So what follows may be considered a rough sketch of "American cuisine" c. 1960. I write mostly in the past tense, as our understanding of what is "American" has become considerably more contested in the past few decades, although much of this still applies to broad segments of what is sometimes called Middle America (Levenstein 1988, Pillsbury 1998, McWilliams 2005).

Basic Foods: In keeping with its Anglo-heritage, American cuisine put meat, especially beef, at the center of the plate, while "starch" was considered to be a wrapper or side dish and vegetables mere embroidery. The Spanish, too, prioritized meat and wheat, pushing indigenous maize, legumes, and produce to the side (Pilcher 1998). As meat and dairy products have long been cheaper and more available in America than elsewhere—thanks in large part to the huge government subsidies devoted to replacing native grasses, buffalo, and Indians with corn, cows, and cowboys—almost all immigrants have added prodigious amounts of animal foods to their Old World cuisines (Diner 2001). Ratifying and rationalizing their tastes, Americans still consider animal protein to be essential for proper nutrition. Reflecting the New Nutrition of the early twentieth century (Levenstein 1988) vegetables became "good for you" but were considered "boring" and not "filling," except perhaps for salads, corn, and potatoes slathered in animal fats. At the high point of WASP hegemony, the emblematic vegetable dish was a mixture of finely chopped raw vegetables molded—indeed imprisoned—in plain gelatin, a byproduct of the slaughterhouses. According to food writer Laura Shapiro, this "perfection salad," was "the very image of a salad at last in control of itself" (1986: 100). This compulsion to encase the vegetable within the animal endures in the Jell-O cookery that is the pride of much Middle American cuisine. Conversely, the belief that a grain-centered diet is inadequate and perhaps even dangerous persists in the belief that "starches" are fattening, and thus out of control.

Flavor Principles: Genteel Americans long disdained certain strong spices—especially garlic and hot peppers—perhaps because they were too closely associated with lower-class immigrants, or perhaps because, Farb and Armelagos speculate, blandness served as a common denominator in a highly pluralistic society. Here again, the British heritage mattered, for eighteenth-century French philosopher Voltaire allegedly sniped that England was a nation of "sixty different religions but only one sauce" (Egerton 1994: 44). Valuing "honesty" and "sincerity," colonists suspected sauces of inherent elitism, especially of the upper-class French variety (Kaufman 2004: 403). To be sure American gentry loved a crude version of French food even in the early republican period, and the taste for complex spices has expanded much in recent years. Even so, the process of "Americanization" today still resembles the way Victorians absorbed a few "foreign foods," such as "Hindoo" curries and Chinese "chop suey"—by "blunting, the flavors and dismantling the complications" (Shapiro 1986: 213).

In keeping with their traditional wariness of Old World cuisines, modernistic Americans were quick to accept canned, frozen, and otherwise processed foods, but only by being convinced through advertising and branding that they were somehow "fresh" and "natural." (In this way the modern was reconciled with the traditional.) Among the main criteria for "freshness" in North American cuisine:

- Packaged bread should be "soft." Firm, chewy bread was considered "stale" (unless toasted).
- Vegetables must have certain predictable colors, generally "bright." Tomatoes, strawberries, and apples must be a certain shade of red; carrots and oranges, orange; string

beans, peppers, and squash, green; bananas, yellow. Similar color standards applied to animal foods, e.g., yellow butter, margarine, and chicken, "red" meat. To achieve these colors, certain genetic strains were favored, and as a last resort dyes and waxes might be added. (Here again, modernistic means were employed to achieve "traditional" ends.)

- Sweetness was equated with freshness, hence the addition of sugar to most processed foods. And extra sodium perked up tired canned and frozen foods, restoring some of the "natural" flavor lost somewhere along the extended food chain.

- For drinks: the colder the better. "Keep it cold, keep it fresh." Room-temperature ales might be considered highly drinkable in Britain but were considered "flat" in America. Only an extravagantly affluent society could afford such widespread and extreme refrigeration. (Convenience thus reinforced taste.) Cheap refrigeration also shaped the American preference for dry-aged refrigerated beef—thought to be more "tender" (or at least softer) than freshly killed meat (Pilcher 2006: 10–11). At the same time, reflecting the same abundance of fossil fuels, "hot" meals had to be *really* hot—no lukewarm street foods here. Coffee and tea had to be either "iced" or boiled.

- Given the growing distance between real farms and urban markets, consumers were easily assured of a product's freshness by advertisements that depicted stereotypical, Disneyesque farm scenes of ruggedly hearty family farmers, well-groomed, pest-free fields, and contented cattle, piglets, and chickens running free in sanitary barnyards.

- As in many cultures, whiteness was long considered a mark of refinement, sophistication, and cultivation. Darker foods were considered more crude, primitive, and undesirable. In recent decades, however, health-conscious elites have reversed such associations to the extent that heavy, dark "peasant breads" are now marketed largely to the more affluent segments of the population, while white bread has more populistic appeal (Belasco 2006b: 48–50).

Since such generalizations are so broad and open to exception, it is also possible to "read" a cuisine by an intense analysis of a single favorite food. Take the Oreo, one of America's best-selling, most cherished brands. Over 360 billion of these three-layer cookies have been sold since 1912. Reading the label reveals certain prominent ingredients in the industrial diet (basic foods): refined flour, sugar, assorted vegetable oils, artificial flavors, stabilizers, preservatives, a dash of sodium, and the common denominator—maize, especially corn starch and high-fructose corn syrup (Pollan 2006: 15–119). Chocolate comes last on the label and thus constitutes the smallest ingredient—a little goes a long way. "Freshness" is asserted by the plastic wrapping as well as by the Nabisco trademark imprinted on every cookie and cracker—a symbol originating with the fifteenth-century Venetian Society of Printers and signifying "the triumph of the moral and spiritual over the evil and material." The Oreo's sculpted Maltese Cross pattern—emblem of medieval Christian warriors—further conveys a sense of loyalty, trust, honesty, and bravery. If there is a flavor principle, it is ultra-sweet, with a smear of fat (the white layer). We taste as much with our eyes as our tongues, so visual appearance is also important. The cookie's ornate carvings and fluted edges combine with the red, white, and blue packaging to convey a festive, quasi-nationalistic feeling. Stark contrasts of color (deep brown; bright white) and texture (crunchy outer layers; soft filling) also sharpen the taste appeal. An accompanying glass of milk cuts the sweetness and clears the teeth of dark crumbs. In keeping with the corporate-industrial-global nature of the American food system, the manipulative techniques that produce and preserve this pastry, and the infrastructure that supplies it, are elaborate, energy-intensive, and opaque. The cookie's cocoa and palm oil alone may travel halfway around the world.

The Oreo isn't all about business, however. As corporate, globalized, and mass-marketed as it is, the Oreo also lends itself to highly individualized consumption "protocols"—as suggested in folklorist Elizabeth Adler's food studies classic, "Creative Eating: The Oreo Syndrome" (1983). We don't all eat the same food in the same way. Rather, Oreo consumers tend to divide between those who carefully take it apart first and eat each layer separately (twisters) and those who crunch all three layers together (nibblers), as well as between those who like to "dunk" their cookie in milk and those who like it dry. While these differences may seem trivial, Adler's point is that people like to play with their food, and this is also seen in the varied approaches to eating a fried egg. "Not only do we ritualize our style of eating, we tend to separate foods that are combined. "We take apart the Oreo; we eat first the white, then the yolk, of a fried egg. By attempting this separation, we create a risk, accepting a challenge to prove our control over food whose fragile quality makes it easily destructible" (5). Similar variations apply to the way we eat corn, fried potatoes, gravy and biscuits, pancakes, animal crackers (appendages first?), and entire meals. "Do you eat foods one at a time, first all the vegetables, then all the meat, then all the starches? Or do you eat a bit from each group, working your way around the plate in a circular fashion until all is gone? Do you eat your salad first, last, or with the meal? Do you drink milk or other liquids throughout the meal or gulp them down all at once at the end?" (7). Resisting the standardization and homogeneity of modern life, people like to "customize" their eating to suit personal needs and preferences. Adler suggests that those who carefully twist off all the layers and eat the sweetest one last may be categorized as "neat eaters" who like to delay gratification, while those who simply crunch the whole cookie at once are more impulsive and impatient. Pointing to some highly impressionistic demography, Nabisco's own market research claims Chicago and Philadelphia tend to be "dunking towns", while New York and Las Vegas are "twisting towns." And in an illustration of how new media technologies have enhanced customization, entire websites are devoted to discussions of how to eat Oreos and what that means. Aiming to control and "unlock the magic" of Oreo consumption, Nabisco even maintains one of the most popular fan sites. Similar forums—some corporate, some consumer-based (or "vernacular")—exist for other mass-market icons, such as Jell-O, Twinkies, Coca-Cola, and Velveeta.

Personalization also applies to the way we *think* about common foods. While the Oreo may be a highly predictable "cash cow" for Nabisco and its owner, Kraft Foods, for the individual consumer it may evoke acutely poignant childhood. In "Ode to Oreos," *San Francisco Chronicle* columnist Adair Lara recalls her childhood in Marin County, California, in the 1960s: "Mother sang along to 'Steam Heat' on the record player, my sister practiced with her Hula-Hoop, and I was in love with the taste and smell and look of everything." Ask a hundred people, "What do you think of when you eat an Oreo?" and you may get a hundred different answers, some intensely nostalgic, others painful, as in the student who will always associate Oreos with throwing up in the back seat during one particularly long and stressful family outing. And in a subversive appropriation of the brand name, the word "Oreo" has also been used by some African-Americans to criticize assimilationists who are "black on the outside, white on the inside." Needless to say, such usages do not appear on Nabisco's official "Oreo and Milk Memories" site.

The ability of particular foods to spark powerful personal recollections and associations leads us to another key concept of food studies: we are what we *ate*.

MADELEINES: FOOD AND MEMORY

For the connection between food and memory we inevitably turn to a very famous passage from the first volume of Marcel Proust's *Remembrance of Things Past*, Book I (1934: 34). Visiting his mother's home in the French village of Combray, Proust's stand-in protagonist Swann absent-mindedly dips a small, fluted cookie called a *madeleine* in his mother's tea. The experience is magical.

> No sooner had the warm liquid, and the crumbs with it, touched my palate than a shudder ran through my whole body, and I stopped, intent upon the extraordinary changes that were taking place. An exquisite pleasure had invaded my senses, but individual, detached, with no suggestion of its origin. And at once the vicissitudes of life had become indifferent to me, its disasters innocuous, its brevity illusory—this new sensation having had on me the effect which love has of filling me with a precious essence; or rather this essence was not in me, it was myself. I had ceased to feel mediocre, accidental, mortal. Whence could it have come to me, this all-powerful joy? I was conscious that it was connected with the taste of tea and cake, but that it infinitely transcended those savors, could not, indeed, be of the same nature as theirs. Where did it come from? What did it signify? How could I seize upon and define it? …
>
> And suddenly the memory returned. The taste was that of the little crumb of madeleine which on Sunday mornings at Combray, … my aunt Leonie used to give me, dipping it first in her own cup of lime-flower tea. And once I had recognized the taste of the … madeleine soaked in her decoction of lime-flowers

... , immediately the old grey house ... rose up like the scenery of a theater to attach itself to the little pavilion, opening on to the garden, which had been built out behind it for my parents and with the house the town ... the Square, where I was sent before luncheon, the streets along which I used to run errands, the country roads we took when it was fine. And just as the Japanese amuse themselves by filling a porcelain bowl with water and steeping in it little crumbs of paper which until then are without character or form, but, the moment they become wet, stretch themselves and bend, take on color and distinctive shape, that moment all the flowers in our garden and in M. Swarm's park, and the water-lilies on the Vivonne and the good folk of the village and their little dwellings and the parish church and the whole of Combray and of its surroundings, taking their proper shapes and growing solid, sprang into being, towns and gardens alike, from my cup of tea.

Proust's chance encounter proved unusually fruitful—seven volumes of fictionalized recollections. While few can be so productive, almost anyone can write a short vignette based on their personal madeleines. Some stories will be sweet, some sour, and some bittersweet. For example, I ask students to write 500 words about their own madeleines. For some, powerful food memories spring immediately into mind, while others need to await some serendipitous meeting—say, a distinctive aroma encountered when entering a friend's home. Either way, the stories amply illustrate the various ways that eating reveals who we are—and are not.

For such young people these students are already profoundly nostalgic for pre-adolescent childhood. "Grandma madeleines" prevail. One writer's taste of cornbread conjures up thoughts of her annual visits to her now departed grandparents in the rural South. "The summers spent in Alabama seem like a lifetime ago but the memories remain in my mind as if they occurred yesterday: ... swimming at the local pool and beach, going to the movies, go-kart racing, and eating the best food that I have eaten in my life." Another African-American student recalls her grandmother's special Sunday dinners—barbecued spareribs, baked macaroni and cheese, collard greens, and, again, cornbread—consumed avidly after church and, in the fall at least, during Washington Redskins' football games. "Those were the best times of my life and all it takes is one bite of macaroni to take me back." Such recollections transcend national boundaries, as a taste of coconut chicken curry reminds one student of "my childhood in India, brought me sweet memories of my grandmother, Indian summers, power failures, good friends and the meals I looked forward to from school." Making *cafecito* [strong Cuban coffee with milk] in her dorm room returns another student to her Miami roots: "Cuban coffee provides the vehicle that allows the Cuban exile community to gather to sip the brew and discuss the anger, the mourning and painful yearning for a country in chains. It was through a simple cafecito with my dad and grandfather every Saturday and Sunday morning at the omnipresent coffee stand, hearing stories of Cuba, that help shape my identity as a Cuban."

Box 2.2. Madeleines: We Are What We Ate

Food is more than an amalgam of biochemical nutrients. What we eat has enormous significance as a medium for personal recollection and collective identity. In this exercise, you are asked to reflect on a food that is especially laden with emotional, autobiographical, and symbolic meaning to you—your equivalent of the tiny cake (madeleine) that sparked French novelist Marcel Proust's seven-volume classic, *Remembrance of Things Past* (1913–1926).

Read the Proust excerpt, then think hard about your own personal madeleine. It may be anything—from a full meal to a packaged snack—as long as it's edible. Try to taste it before writing. In 500 words, describe your madeleine and the images, associations, and memories it conjures up. These images do not have to be positive, by the way. Describe, also, how you encountered this memory—for example, by chance, or by will.

You can also try classifying your madeleine:

- Is it positive, negative, or somewhere in between (bittersweet)?
- Is it a comfort food or a discomfort food? A medium for conflict or reunion?
- Is it homemade or commercial?
- Is it a demographic "marker" of ethnicity, region, generation, gender, religion, or class?
- Does eating this food make you part of a group? Exclude you from other groups? (Boundary maintenance)

Note: If you can't come up with your own special madeleine, try the Oreo exercise described earlier in this selection: "When I eat an Oreo I think of …"

For further examples of the creative use of food memories: Sutton 2001, Winegardner 1998, Reichl 1998, Boorstin 2002, Friedensohn 2006, Abu-Jaber 2005.

Many stories involve similarly strong ethnic or regional "markers"—Chesapeake Bay crabs and oysters, Philadelphia cheesesteaks, boardwalk fries, baklava, kielbasa, goulash, schnitzel, chutney, pierogi, pizzelles, tamales, *puerco asado y arroz con frijoles, banh cuon* (Vietnamese dumplings), Korean fried fish. What makes these particularly poignant is that, when filtered through the lens of nostalgia, such memories become a way of preserving identities now perceived to be endangered by migration, mobility, and suburban mass culture.

Only a few actually welcome change, and for them the passage to adulthood may again be represented through a particular meal—as in one student's first experience (aged eighteen) with sushi, which signified both the transition to adult tastes and the high cost of such treats: "Well, the first time I ate sushi, I was ruined. It was orgasmic; even better. I knew when I took that bite of tuna that I was forever destined to a life of knowing, but not always having. (Sushi is very expensive.)" As in Eden, tasting the fruit of knowledge meant Paradise Lost. "Like the Aristotelian prisoner in the cave, I was shown a glimpse of heaven, and then led back to the world I of men, where beefburgers and buffalo wings were king." A similar story relates how a college student's current binges with cheap beer pale in comparison with his first sip of alcohol—a particularly expensive brand of vodka. And another's encounter with pasta recalls an eye-opening, mouth-watering semester abroad in Rome; where fine food and a healthier, pedestrian-oriented lifestyle contrasted sharply with the car-based fast food diet of his youth; after Rome, returning to suburban America, was difficult indeed.

Given that one's first conscious experience is usually at the maternal breast (or bottle), mother-related madeleines seem less likely to evoke a particular place or event than an ongoing process of parental nurturing. Just as Proust's mother offered tea and cookies to warm him up on a chilly day, mothers often prepare special foods for sick children, and these may become the "comfort foods" of adulthood—chicken soup, orange sherbet, cinnamon toast, plain rice, scrambled eggs, soft-boiled eggs cracked with a teaspoon and with white bread to dunk. Eggs seem particularly evocative this way—a reflection perhaps of their reproductive significance. Missing the small routines of childhood, some recall the foods eaten often—such as the peanut butter and jelly sandwich, or the simple *milch reis* (milk and rice) prepared by Mom and consumed every day for many years. Especially moving is the soldier's request for Mom's familiar mashed potatoes on the eve of his departure to Baghdad. Dads, too, are remembered for their recurrent feeding rituals—such as weekend pancakes, barbecues, post-game visits to McDonald's.

More bittersweet is the wistful association of the smell of cooked cabbage with a stern boarding school to which one writer and her sisters had been confined when their mother became gravely ill. And yet, she also finds that these memories "are not disturbing. What is so remarkable is the clarity of these old events, so much so that my sisters and I have been exchanging these thoughts from our past, bringing to mind old promises, feelings and bonds of sisterly love." A literary form of commensality, shared food memories overcome distance and reinforce relationships—perhaps one reason for the popularity of food memoirs.

Some are distinctly sour and establish borders, not bonds. Recently finding herself "incapacitated" by the aroma of stuffed peppers at a friend's house, one writer is transported back to a traumatic dinner of early childhood, when she balked at eating her father's special dish of rice, tomatoes, and beef—the same combination in the stuffed peppers. "Little girl," her father threatened, "if you don't eat it, you'll wear it!" and he then proceeded to dump the full plate on her head. Although she subsequently forgave her parents "for the cruel and unusual punishments they inflict on us," such incidents remind us that the family dinner table can be as much an arena for rebellion as for reunion. Along the same lines, another student's story begins with nostalgia for the aroma of Mom's cold-weather chili but then goes on to remember that, for some reason, whether digestive or cognitive, chili has always made her sick—signaling her separation, even alienation, from the rest of the family. Fixing boundaries, food reminds us of who we are *not*, as when one writer visits her spouse's Greek family and commits the "major taste-testing faux pas" of eating the bitter cloves holding his grandmother's baklava together; only an insider would know that the cloves are to be removed before biting.

Given the American antipathy to "healthy" vegetables, many negative memories involve childhood resistance to spinach, broccoli, squash, lima beans, peas, and okra. Conversely, vegetarians who reject meat at the family dinner table recall even stronger stigmatization, at least at first. Reporting on familial conflicts over meat, folklorist LuAnne K. Roth writes, "If patriotism is indeed 'the love of the good things we ate in our childhood,' as [Chinese writer, 1895–1976] Lin Yutang remarks, then it makes sense that vegetarians are initially perceived by their families to be unpatriotic, un-American, and even downright un-family like" (Roth 2005: 188). One suspects that vegetarians receive similar reactions in other carnivorous cultures as well. Noting how vegetarians can be inconvenient dinner guests, journalist Michael Pollan finds himself "inclined to agree with the French, who gaze upon any personal dietary prohibition as bad manners" (2006: 314). But historically, such "manners" are relatively recent, especially in ordinary homes, where children were generally ignored until the nineteenth century, when they became the object of more moralistic "nutritional policing" by anxious bourgeois families, by would-be reformers, and by the state itself (Coveney 2006). The intensity of family meal memories is both a product of modernity, as well as a reaction to it.

Sometimes modernity itself is the stuff of nostalgia. Akin to the way different people eat and perceive Oreos, some mass-marketed convenience foods become the subject of customized recollections: a Velveeta cheese sandwich consumed on road trips in an old VW bus to Grateful Dead concerts; an "Archway molasses cookie" purchased to reward a four-year-old for getting up early to help her now divorced father cook breakfast; a simple Handy Snack (four crackers packaged with cheese and a red stick for spreading it) routinely shared with a beloved grandfather while playing cards; or a 7-Eleven slushie bought *on the way* to grandma's. It is the cheap, artificially-flavored crushed ice, not grandma's home cooking, that sparks this memory. For one writer, the unorthodox blend of Lay's potato chips and plain cottage cheese recalls visits to grandma, who claims to have invented this family snack. (According to market researchers Brian Wansink and Cynthia Sangerman, 2000, potato chips are America's favorite comfort food.) For a former Little Leaguer, Gatorade evokes "old teammates, hot summer days, triple headers, harsh defeats, and brilliant victories." In an R-rated version, the "pop" of Gatorade's "freshness seal" suggests trips with high school friends to the beach, where—in a taste of the complex sexual rituals of teenage boys—they drank massive amounts of Citrus Cooler as a purported cure for "blue balls" (a euphemism for painfully unconsummated male sexual arousal). And, belying the conventional wisdom that mass culture endangers family life, students warmly recall the mass-produced foods eaten with family members while watching television together. Eating normally proscribed "junk foods" on sick days while watching daytime TV is another common memory.

Given the mind-bending power of madeleines, it is inevitable that some have attempted to channel those memories toward social goals more "significant than merely fulfilling a professor's assignment or selling a memoir. In *Remembrance of Repasts: An Anthropology of Food and Memory* (2001), David Sutton shows how Greek islanders plan elaborate feasts with the conscious goal of having them remembered collectively later on; conversely their keen ability to remember and discuss particular meals many years later prolongs the community-building function (commensality) of social eating. In perhaps the grimmest example of how food memories can empower people, starving concentration camp inmates during the Second World War found emotional sustenance by sharing recipes for meals past. In *Memory's Kitchen: A Legacy from the Women of Terezin* (1996), editor Cam De Silva sees such memories as a form of resistance "to those who want to annihilate you and your cultures and traditions, and everything about you … . By writing [them down, the women] were using these as weapons. They were using potato doughnuts and dumplings, and stuffed eggs, and caramels from Bonn, instead of bombs and bazookas" (quoted in Rosofsky 2004: 52). In a variation, affluent descendants of slaves, famine survivors, war refugees, and impoverished immigrants will cherish the stigmatized foods of their oppressive past as a way to honor their ancestors' courage and endurance—for example, the simple but fragrant biscuits of a mill town tenement, the scrounged "hedge nutrition" of Ireland, the "Geechie Rice" of the Sea Islands, the unleavened bread of the Jewish Exodus, the boiled chicken feet of Chinese peasants (Avakian 1997). And remembering even the most distasteful foods of the past may have some survival value. Lacking many of the genetically programmed "instincts" of the more selective species, omnivores may employ memories as a way to distinguish the harmful from the wholesome. The longer the memory, the longer the life (Pollan 2006: 287–298).

Madeleines can also be exploited for commercial purposes. Whether in Disney World or Bali, the vacation industry is well known for its stereotypical representation of so-called "traditional foods," which have become an essential ingredient in "culinary tourism" (Long 2003, Halter 2000, Heldke 2003). Anthropologist Richard Wilk shows that a distinctively "Belizean" cuisine emerged not so much from the ordinary citizens of Belize—an exceptionally multicultural society—as from the pressure of nostalgic expatriates and authenticity-seeking travelers (2002, 2006). A somewhat similar dynamic is seen in anthropologist Carla Guerron-Montero's study of the Bocas del Toro region of Panama, where locals learned to serve the Spanish-style meals that tourists expected, rather than the very different Afro-Antillean cuisine of the area (2004). Attempting to cash in on "heritage tourism," the declining industrial city of Pueblo, Colorado built a new identity around the once despised chili pepper (Haverluk 2002). In a classic study of such "neo-localism," historian Kolleen Guy suggests that the legendary French *terroir* that one supposedly detects in a taste of good Bordeaux or brie was in fact the relatively recent concoction of an opportunistic alliance among nationalist politicians, ambitious growers, and tourist chateau operators all seeking to serve their narrow economic interests while stifling the competition from seemingly less "authentic" locales (2002). An analogous process took place in Victorian America, when descendants of the original British colonists consciously invented the components of the now familiar Thanksgiving dinner—roast turkey, stuffing, pumpkin pie—as a way to assert their superiority to newcomers who arrived with radically different cultures and cuisines (Smith 2004).

Similarly, advertisements for McDonald's, Frosted Flakes, Kraft Macaroni and Cheese, and Kool-Aid may take advantage of childhood associations with processed foods to build loyalty for their brands (and for industrial food in general). Such associations "work" best if they tap dominant myths. According to its advertising, a bite of sausage at Bob Evans's Farm Restaurant "takes me back home"—but only if my home resembles a Currier and Ives print of a prosperous Ohio farmstead. And, as we have seen, Nabisco even has a website where consumers of Oreos—the national madeleine?—can exchange their memories, but only the positive ones. One does wonder about whether such mass-mediated recollections will further homogenize the modern mind, producing "McMemories." Yet just as the playing of a "golden oldie" song may spark vastly different recollections of teenage life, so too may consumers experience and recall a Big Mac and fries in very specialized ways. A similar "localization" occurs in the way specific cultures view and reinterpret globalized fast foods: a Big Mac in Beijing may "mean" something quite different from a Big Mac in Chicago (Watson 1997). Similarly, Tim Horton donuts are prized as an ironic emblem of Canadian national identity precisely because they seem "simple," "humble," and thus un-American, even though they are now massif; produced by Wendy's, an American corporation (Penfold 2002).

Along with imparting meaning to our daily lives, these rich linkages between food and identity pose major challenges to those who worry about responsibility—the costs and consequences of what we eat. If pot roast, bacon-laden collards, or chicken curry recall Grandma, it becomes hard to see much evil in the animal industry if a Happy Meal or pizza reminds us of dinner with Dad after the soccer match, then rejecting fat means rejecting Dad. The same might be said of a post-hockey game Tim Horton donut, sugar and trans fats notwithstanding. Can we really label Grandma and Dad "irresponsible" and "deadbeats"? If Nabisco is beloved for its Oreos, can we really be angry at its former corporate parent, Philip Morris? By renaming its food divisions Altria (with the same word root as "altruism"), Philip Morris certainly hoped to obscure its identity as a tobacco marketer.

Further difficulties result from the uncertain nature of identity in a mobile, multicultural world. If "we are what we eat," who are "we" anyway? How many people does it take to comprise a "we"? And in what context? As voters? As soldiers? Cooks? Customers? Do we define a group's identity by bioregion, by foodshed, by arbitrary lines drawn on an inaccurate map two hundred years ago by imperial politicians, by the selective recollections of aging immigrants? An especially vivid example of the last difficulty can be seen in Barry Levinson's film, *Avalon* (1990), which traces the progress of a large Baltimore Jewish family through three generations. In an early scene, the extended immigrant family crowds a small row house for a Thanksgiving feast. While the family has no interest in the holiday's Anglo-American history, they do value this annual ritual as an opportunity to remember the old country and their early struggles in America. Yet the fallibility of memory is accentuated in a disagreement over whether one crucial event—the arrival of the family's patriarch—took place in midsummer or midwinter. As if to emphasize the subjectivity of remembrances, Levinson reenacts The Fathers arrival twice, in both seasons. Moreover, to demonstrate the elusiveness of memory in a culture that values youth above age, the Thanksgiving gatherings become increasingly contentious over the years, as the children grow impatient with their elders' stories. Near the end a much smaller nuclear family—a mere sliver of the original clan—is seen eating its dinner in silence, in front of the TV. Perhaps to be an American is to forget, *not* remember. To be sure, memory, like taste, may fade with age everywhere. In *Ang Lee's Eat Drink Man "Woman* (1994), a retired Taiwanese chef attempts to keep his splintering family together by cooking elaborate Sunday banquets, only to discover that he has lost his ability to taste. Rather than binding his daughters with pleasant tastes of the past, his nearly inedible dishes almost drive them away.

And what about the phrase "what we eat"? We eat so many different foods! Which ones signify deep identity and which simply fill us up? Culinarians like to draw deep distinctions between human "dining," which is full of deep cultural significance, and animal "feeding," a purely biological act, but not everything we eat has a lot of meaning. Sometimes we just "feed." And then there is that troublesome identity verb "are," derived from "to be." What is identity anyway? Can we even be sure of our own personality or "character," much less the defining qualities of broader entities such as "neighborhood," "region," or "nation"? What about those of us who come from several different ethnic or racial backgrounds? In an affecting study of Korean-American adoptees, social worker Kathleen Ja Sook Berquist finds people caught between markers—not really Asian, not fully American either. When well-meaning white parents attempt to cultivate their children's Korean identity with iconic foods such as kim chee, moon cakes, and bulgogi, the adoptees may come away feeling even more alienated. "Food as an access point creates an awareness of the estranged position adoptees find themselves in and the incompleteness of their cultural memory. Instead of feeding a hunger [for identity], it exposes a void" (2006: 150). Sometimes people may feel most "whole," most like "themselves," over neutral food. For example, in Spike

Lee's *Jungle Fever* (1991), a mixed race New York couple escapes from equally intolerant Bensonhurst (Italian) and Harlem (African-American) by sharing takeout Chinese food in blandly corporate midtown Manhattan. Similarly, sociologists Gaye Tuchman and Harry Gene Levine argue that second generation Jewish New Yorkers took to Chinese food because it seemed so "cosmopolitan, urbane, and sophisticated"—i.e., less confining or "provincial" than the kosher Eastern European fare of their parents (1993: 164). And anthropologist James Watson writes that the Chinese youth of Hong Kong embraced McDonald's, "precisely because it was not Chinese"; that is it seemed more "laid-back" and "non-hierarchical" (Watson 1997: 86). In all, we don't always want to eat "what we are."

What if Walt Whitman's "Song of Myself" was right in claiming that the self is so full of contradictions and uncertainties as to be "not a bit tamed" and ultimately "untranslatable"? It doesn't take psychoanalysis or romantic poetry, to tell us that if our personal identities are so elusive, our collective affiliations must be much more so. And the confusion does not apply to just modern or postmodern cuisines. Richard Wilk has shown that ever since the first pirates arrived in the sixteenth century, Belizean food practices have been "heterogeneous, polyglot, disorderly, and even incoherent"—an apt description, perhaps, of human cuisines in general (2002: 79).

So, returning to our original culinary triangle, we may find that deciding what to eat maybe complicated not only by considerations of convenience and responsibility, but also by conflicts within identity itself.

THE MAN WHO ATE EVERYTHING

By Jeffrey Steingarten

"M y first impulse was to fall upon the cook," wrote Edmondo de Amicis, a nineteenth-century traveler to Morocco. "In an instant I understood perfectly how a race who ate such food must necessarily believe in another God and hold essentially different views of human life from our own. … There was a suggestion of soap, wax, pomatum, of unguents, dyes, cosmetics; of everything, in short, most unsuited to enter a human mouth."

This is precisely how I felt about a whole range of foods, particularly desserts in Indian restaurants, until 1989, the year that I, then a lawyer was appointed food critic of *Vogue* magazine. As I considered the awesome responsibilities of my new post, I grew morose. For I, like everybody I knew, suffered from a set of powerful, arbitrary, and debilitating attractions and aversions at mealtime. I feared that I could be no more objective than an art critic who detests the color yellow or suffers from red-green color blindness. At the time I was friendly with a respected and powerful editor of cookbooks who grew so nauseated by the flavor of cilantro that she brought a pair of tweezers to Mexican and Indian restaurants and pinched out every last scrap of it before she would take a bite. Imagine the dozens of potential Julia Childs and M. F. K. Fishers whose books she peevishly rejected, whose careers she snuffed in their infancy! I vowed not to follow in her footsteps.

Suddenly, intense food preferences, whether phobias or cravings, struck me as the most serious of all personal limitations. That very day I sketched out a Six-Step Program to liberate my palate and my soul. No smells or tastes are innately repulsive, I assured myself, and what's learned can be forgot.

STEP ONE was to compose an annotated list.

My Food Phobias

1. Foods I wouldn't touch, even if I were starving on a desert island:

None, except maybe insects. Many cultures find insects highly nutritious and love their crunchy texture. The pre-Hispanic Aztecs roasted worms in a variety of ways and made pressed caviar from mosquito eggs. This proves that no innate human programming keeps me from eating them, too. Objectively, I must look as foolish as those Kalahari Bushmen who face famine every few years because they refuse to eat three-quarters of the 223 animal species around them. I will deal with this phobia when I have polished off the easy ones.

2. Foods I wouldn't touch even if I were starving on a desert island until absolutely everything else runs out:

Kimchi, the national pickle of Korea. Cabbage, ginger, garlic, and red peppers—I love them all, but not when they are fermented together for many months to become kimchi. Nearly forty-one million South Koreans eat kimchi three times a day. They say "kimchi" instead of "cheese" when someone is taking their picture. I say, "Hold the kimchi."

Anything featuring dill. What could be more benign than dill?

Swordfish. This is a favorite among the feed-to-succeed set, who like it grilled to the consistency of running shoes and believe it is good for them. A friend of mine eats swordfish five times a week and denies that he has any food phobias. Who's kidding whom? Returning obsessively to a few foods is the same as being phobic toward all the rest. This may explain the Comfort Food Craze. But the goal of the arts, culinary or otherwise, is not to increase our comfort. That is the goal of an easy chair.

During my own praline period, which lasted for three years, I would order any dessert on the menu containing caramelized hazelnuts and ignore the rest. I grew so obsessive that I almost missed out on the créme brûlée craze then sweeping the country. After my praline period had ebbed, I slid into a créme brûlée fixation, from which I forcibly wrenched myself only six months ago.

Anchovies. I met my first anchovy on a pizza in 1962, and it was seven years before I mustered the courage to go near another. I am known to cross the street whenever I see an anchovy coming. Why would anybody consciously choose to eat a tiny, oil-soaked, leathery maroon strip of rank and briny flesh?

Lard. The very word causes my throat to constrict and beads of sweat to appear on my forehead.

Desserts in Indian restaurants. The taste and texture of face creams belong in the boudoir, not on the plate. See above.

Also: miso, mocha, chutney, raw sea urchins, and falafel (those hard, dry, fried little balls of ground chickpeas unaccountably enjoyed in Middle Eastern countries).

3. Foods I might eat if I were starving on a desert island but only if the refrigerator were filled with nothing but chutney, sea urchins, and falafel:

Greek food. I have always considered "Greek cuisine" an oxymoron. Nations are like people. Some are good at cooking while others have a talent for music or baseball or manufacturing memory chips. The Greeks are really good at both pre-Socratic philosophy and white statues. They have not been good cooks since the fifth century B.C., when Siracusa on Sicily was the gastronomic capital of the world. Typical of modern-day Greek cuisine are feta cheese and retsina wine. Any country that pickles its national cheese in brine and adulterates its national wine with pine pitch should order dinner at the local Chinese place and save its energies for other things. The British go to Greece just for the food, which says volumes to me. You would probably think twice before buying an Algerian or Russian television set. I thought for ten years before buying my last Greek meal.

Clams. I feel a mild horror about what goes on in the wet darkness between the shells of all bivalves, but clams are the only ones I dislike. Is it their rubbery consistency or their rank subterranean taste, or is the horror deeper than I know?

Blue food (not counting plums and berries). This may be a rational aversion, because I am fairly sure that God meant the color blue mainly for food that has gone bad.

Also: cranberries, kidneys, okra, millet, coffee ice cream, refried beans, and many forms of yogurt.
This had to stop.

STEP TWO was to immerse myself in the scientific literature on human food selection.

By design and by destiny, humans are omnivores. Our teeth and digestive systems are all-purpose and ready for anything. Our genes do not dictate what foods we should find tasty or repulsive. We come into the world with a yen for sweets (newborns can even distinguish among glucose, fructose, lactose, and sucrose) and a weak aversion to bitterness, and after four months develop a fondness for salt. Some people are born particularly sensitive to one taste or odor; others have trouble digesting milk sugar or wheat gluten. A tiny fraction of adults, between 1 and 2 percent, have true (and truly dangerous) food allergies. All human cultures consider fur, paper, and hair inappropriate as food.

And that's about it. Everything else is *learned*. Newborns are not repelled even by the sight and smell of putrefied meat crawling with maggots.

The nifty thing about being omnivores is that we can take nourishment from an endless variety of flora and fauna and easily adapt to a changing world—crop failures, droughts, herd migrations, restaurant closings, and the like. Lions and tigers will starve in a salad bar, as will cows in a steak house, but not us. Unlike cows, who remain well nourished eating only grass, humans *need* a great diversity of foods to stay healthy.

Yet by the age of twelve, we all suffer from a haphazard collection of food aversions ranging from revulsion to indifference. The tricky part about being omnivores is that we are always in danger of poisoning ourselves. Catfish have taste buds on their whiskers, but we are not so lucky. Instead, we are born with a cautious ambivalence toward novel foods, a precarious balance between neophilia and neophobia. Just one bad stomach ache or attack of nausea after dinner is enough to form a potent aversion—even if the food we ate did not actually cause the problem and even if we know it didn't. Hives or rashes may lead us rationally to avoid the food that caused them, but only an upset stomach and nausea will result in a lasting, irrational, lifelong sense of disgust. Otherwise, psychologists know very little about the host of powerful likes and dislikes—let us lump them all under the term "food phobias"—that children carry into adulthood.

By closing ourselves off from the bounties of nature, we become failed omnivores. We let down the omnivore team. God tells us in the Book of Genesis, right after Noah's flood, to eat everything under the sun. Those who ignore his instructions are no better than godless heathens.

The more I contemplated food phobias, the more I became convinced that people who habitually avoid certifiably delicious foods are at least as troubled as people who avoid sex, or take no pleasure from it, except that the latter will probably seek psychiatric help, while food phobics rationalize their problem in the name of genetic inheritance, allergy, vegetarianism, matters of taste, nutrition, food safety, obesity, or a sensitive nature. The varieties of neurotic food avoidance would fill several volumes, but milk is a good place to start.

Overnight, everybody you meet has become lactose intolerant. It is the chic food fear of the moment. But the truth is that very, very few of us are so seriously afflicted that we cannot drink even a whole glass of milk a day without ill effects. I know several people who have given up cheese to avoid lactose. But fermented cheeses contain no lactose. Lactose is the sugar found in milk; 98 percent of it is drained off with the whey (cheese is made from the curds), and the other 2 percent is quickly consumed by lactic-acid bacteria in the act of fermentation.

Three more examples: People rid their diet of salt (and their food of flavor) to avoid high blood pressure and countless imagined ills. But no more than 8 percent of the population is sensitive to salt. Only *saturated* fat, mainly from animals, has ever been shown to cause heart disease or cancer, yet nutrition writers and Nabisco get rich pandering to the fear of eating any fat at all. The hyperactivity syndrome supposedly caused by white sugar has never, ever, been verified—and not for lack of trying. In the famous New Haven study, it was the presence of the parents, not the presence of white sugar, that was causing the problem; most of the kids calmed down when their parents left the room.*

I cannot figure out why, but the atmosphere in America today rewards this sort of self-deception. Fear and suspicion of food have become the norm. Convivial dinners have nearly disappeared and with them the sense of festivity and exchange, of community and sacrament. People should be deeply ashamed of the irrational food phobias that keep them from sharing food with each other. Instead, they have become proud and isolated, arrogant and aggressively misinformed.

But not me.

STEP THREE was to choose my weapon. Food phobias can be extinguished in five ways. Which one would work best for me?

Brain surgery. Bilateral lesions made in the basolateral region of the amygdala seem to do the trick in rats and, I think, monkeys—eliminating old aversions, preventing the formation of new ones, and increasing the animals' acceptance of novel foods. But the literature does not report whether having a brain operation also diminishes their ability to, say, follow a recipe. If these experimental animals could talk, would they still be able to? Any volunteers?

Starvation. As Aristotle claimed and modern science has confirmed, any food tastes better the hungrier you are. But as I recently confessed to my doctor, who warned me to take some pill only on an empty stomach, the last time I had an empty stomach was in 1978. He scribbled "hyperphagia" on my chart, your doctor's name for making a spectacle of yourself at the table. He is a jogger.

Bonbons. Why not reward myself with a delectable little chocolate every time I successfully polish off an anchovy, a dish of kimchi, or a bowl of miso soup? Parents have used rewards ever since spinach was discovered. Offering children more playtime for eating dark leafy greens may temporarily work. But offering children an extra Milky Way bar in return for

---

* For the details, be sure to read the chapters "Salt," "Pain Without Gain," and "Murder, My Sweet," in Part Three.

eating more spinach has perverse results: the spinach grows more repellent and the Milky Way more desired.

Drug dependence. Finicky laboratory animals find new foods more palatable after a dose of chlordiazepoxide. According to an old *Physicians' Desk Reference*, this is nothing but Librium, the once-popular tranquilizer, also bottled as Reposans and Sereen. The label warns you about nausea, depression, and operating heavy machinery, I just said no.

Exposure, plain and simple. Scientists tell us that aversions fade away when we eat moderate doses of the hated foods at moderate intervals, especially if the food is complex and new to us. (Don't try this with allergies, but don't cheat either: few of us have genuine food allergies.) Exposure works by overcoming our innate neophobia, the omnivore's fear of new foods that balances the biological urge to explore for them. Did you know that babies who are breast-fed will later have less trouble with novel foods than those who are given formula? The variety of flavors that make their way into breast milk from the mother's diet prepares the infant for the culinary surprises that lie ahead. Most parents give up trying novel foods on their weanlings after two or three attempts and then complain to the pediatrician; this may be the most common cause of fussy eaters and finicky adults—of omnivores manqués. *Most babies will accept nearly anything after eight or ten tries.*

Clearly, mere exposure was the only hope for me.

STEP FOUR was to make eight or ten reservations at Korean restaurants, purchase eight or ten anchovies, search the Zagat guide for eight or ten places with the names Parthenon or Olympia (which I believe are required by statute for Greek restaurants), and bring a pot of water to the boil for cooking eight or ten chickpeas. My plan was simplicity itself: every day for the next six months I would eat at least one food that I detested.

Here are some of the results:

Kimchi. After repeatedly sampling ten of the sixty varieties of kimchi, the national pickle of Korea, kimchi has become my national pickle, too.

Anchovies. I began relating to anchovies a few months ago in northern Italy, where I ordered *bagna caôda* every day—a sauce of garlic, butter, olive oil, and minced anchovies served piping hot over sweet red and yellow peppers as an antipasto in Piemonte. My phobia crumpled when I understood that the anchovies living in American pizza parlors bear no relation to the sweet, tender anchovies of Spain and Italy, cured in dry sea salt and a bit of pepper. Soon I could tell a good *bagna caôda* from a terrific one. On my next trip to Italy I will seek out those fresh charcoal-grilled anchovies of the Adriatic you always hear about.

Clams. My first assault on clams was at a diner called Lunch near the end of Long Island, where I consumed an order of fried bellies and an order of fried strips. My aversion increased sharply.

Eight clams and a few weeks later it was *capellini* in white clam sauce at an excellent southern Italian restaurant around the corner from my house. As I would do so often in the future, even at the expense of my popularity, I urged my companions to cast off their food phobias by ordering at least one dish they expected to detest. If they would go along with my experiment, I would agree to order *nothing* I liked.

All but one agreed, a slim and lovely dancer who protested that her body tells her precisely what to eat and that I am the last person in the universe fit to interfere with those sacred messages. I replied that the innate wisdom of the body is a complete fiction when it comes to omnivores. Soon I had certain proof that my friend was a major closet food phobic when she spent five minutes painstakingly separating her appetizer into two piles. The pile composed of grilled peppers, fennel, and eggplant sat lonely on the plate until her mortified husband and I polished it off. She was so disoriented by either the meal or my unsparing advice that she ate a large handful of potpourri as we waited for our coats.

As for me, the evening was an unqualified success. The white clam sauce was fresh with herbs and lemon and fresh salt air, and my clam phobia was banished in the twinkling of an eye. There is a lot of banal pasta with clam sauce going around these days. If you have a clam phobia, here are two surefire solutions: Order eight to ten white clam pizzas at Frank Pepe's in New Haven, Connecticut, perhaps the single best pizza in the United States and certainly the best thing of any kind in New Haven, Connecticut. Or try the wonderful recipe for linguine with clams and *gremolata* in the *Chez Panisse Pasta, Pizza & Calzone Cookbook* (Random House) once a week for eight consecutive weeks. It is guaranteed to work miracles.

Greek food. My wife, who considers herself, Greek-food-deprived, was on cloud nine when I invited her to our neighborhood Greek restaurant, widely reviewed as the best in the city. As we walked along the street, she hugged me tight like those women in the TV commercials who have just been given a large diamond "for just being you" and launched into a recitation of the only classical Greek she knows, something about the wrath of Achilles. My own mood brightened when I saw that only one retsina befouled the wine list; the other wines were made from aboriginal Greek grapes in Attica or Macedonia or Samos but fermented in the manner of France or California. The dreaded egg-and-lemon soup was nowhere to be seen, and feta was kept mainly in the closet.

We ordered a multitude of appetizers and three main courses. Only the gluey squid, a tough grape leaf that lodged between my teeth, and the Liquid Smoke with which somebody had drenched the roasted eggplant threatened to arouse my slumbering phobia. The rest, most of it simply grilled with lemon and olive oil, was delicious, and as an added bonus I was launched on what still feels like an endless journey toward the acceptance of okra.

Later that evening, my lovely wife was kept up by an upset stomach, and I was kept up by my wife. She swore never to eat Greek food again.

Lard. Paula Wolfert's magnificent *The Cooking of South-West France* (Dial Press) beguiled me into loving lard with her recipe for *confit de porc*—half-pound chunks of fresh pork shoulder flavored with thyme, garlic, cloves, and pepper, poached for three hours in a half gallon of barely simmering lard, and mellowed in crocks of congealed lard for up to four months. When you bring the pork back to life and brown it gently in its own fat, the result is completely delicious, savory, and aromatic. I had never made the dish myself because, following Wolfert's advice, I had always avoided using commercial lard, those one-pound blocks of slightly rank, preservative-filled fat in your butcher's freezer.

Then, one snowy afternoon, I found myself alone in a room with four pounds of pork, an equal amount of pure white pig's fat, and a few hours to spare. Following Wolfert's simple instructions for rendering lard, I chopped up the fat, put it in a deep pot with a little water and some cloves and cinnamon sticks, popped it into a 225-degree oven, and woke up three hours later. After straining out the solids and spices, I was left with a rich, clear golden elixir that perfumed my kitchen, as it will henceforth perfume my life.

Desserts in Indian restaurants. Eight Indian dinners taught me that not every Indian dessert has the texture and taste of face cream. Far from it. Some have the texture and taste of tennis balls. These are named *gulab jamun*, which the menu described as a "light pastry made with dry milk and honey." *Rasmalai* have the texture of day-old bubble gum and refuse to yield to the action of the teeth. On the brighter side, I often finished my *kulfi*, the traditional Indian ice cream, and would love to revisit carrot *halva*, all caramelized and spicy. But I may already have traveled down this road as far as justice requires.

STEP FIVE, final exam and graduation ceremony.

In just six months, I succeeded in purging myself of nearly all repulsions and preferences, in becoming a more perfect omnivore. This became apparent one day in Paris, France—a city to which my arduous professional duties frequently take me. I was trying a nice new restaurant, and when the waiter brought the menu, I found myself in a state unlike any I had ever attained—call it Zen-like if you wish. Everything on the menu, every appetizer, hot and cold, every salad, every fish and bird and piece of meat, was terrifically alluring, but none more than the others. I had absolutely no way of choosing. Though blissful at the prospect of eating, I was unable to order dinner. I was reminded of the medieval church parable of the ass equidistant between two bales of hay, who, because animals lack free will, starves to death. A man, supposedly, would not.

The Catholic Church was dead wrong. I *would* have starved—if my companion had not saved the day by ordering for both of us. I believe I ate a composed salad with slivers of foie gras, a perfect sole meunière, and sweetbreads. Everything was delicious.

STEP SIX, relearning humility. Just because you have become a perfect omnivore does not mean that you must flaunt it. Intoxicated with my own accomplishment, I began to misbehave, especially at dinner parties. When seated next to an especially finicky eater, I would often amuse myself by going straight for the jugular. Sometimes I began slyly by staring slightly too long at the food remaining on her plate and then inquiring whether she would like to borrow my fork. Sometimes I launched a direct assault by asking how long she had had her terror of bread. Sometimes I tricked her by striking up an abstract conversation about allergies. And then I would sit back and complacently listen to her neurotic jumble of excuses and explanations: advice from a personal trainer, intolerance to wheat gluten, a pathetic faith in Dean Ornish, the exquisite—even painful—sensitivity of her taste buds, hints of childhood abuse. And then I would tell her the truth.

I believe that it is the height of compassion and generosity to practice this brand of tough love on dinner-party neighbors who are less omnivorous than oneself. But the perfect omnivore must always keep in mind that, for one to remain omnivorous, it is an absolute necessity to get invited back.

May 1989,
August 1996

Taste

From *Sensation & Perception*

By Jeremy M. Wolfe

Calvin Trillin, a writer who makes wonderful observations about the joys of eating, described his 4-year-old daughter's reaction to "polishing off a particularly satisfying dish of chocolate ice cream." She said, "My tongue is smiling."

What makes tongues smile? As with our noses, the basic answer to this question is molecules. Olfaction and gustation are often grouped together as the chemical senses, and in terms of physiology, these two sensory systems are in some ways quite similar. But the chemicals we taste have already entered our mouths and are about to move even farther into our bodies. Thus, taste serves the most specific function of any of the senses: discerning which chemicals we need to ingest because they are nutritious and which we need to spit out because they may be poisonous. Perhaps this is why something about our liking or disliking of tastes and flavors seems to be very different from the liking or disliking that one might associate with the color red or the sound of middle C on the piano. Nature has equipped us to care passionately about food because that passion holds the key to our survival.

TASTE VERSUS FLAVOR

Before delving any further into the gustatory system, we need to clear up a very old misunderstanding. According to the early Greeks, sensations perceived from foods and beverages in the mouth were tastes, and sensations perceived by sniffing were smells. In fact, however, food molecules are almost always perceived by both our gustatory and our olfactory systems. The molecules we taste are dissolved in our saliva and passed over the taste receptors on our taste buds, as we'll discuss in this chapter. But when we chew and swallow foods, other molecules are released into the air inside our mouths and forced up behind the palate into the nasal cavity, where they contact the olfactory epithelium and stimulate our olfactory receptors (**Figure 14.1**). The brain then knits these **retronasal**

olfactory sensations together with our gustatory sensations into a kind of metasensation that goes by the name **flavor.**

It is quite easy to prevent the airflow that carries odorants through the retronasal passage. Children do it all the time when they hold their noses while eating spinach. Try the following experiment now—but use a piece of chocolate if you're still not crazy about spinach. Pinch your nose before putting the chocolate in your mouth, then chew it and note the sensation, which will be almost pure taste (sweet with a bit of bitter). Then, just before swallowing, release your nose. The volatile molecules responsible for the chocolate sensation will immediately be drawn up behind your palate and into the nasal cavity, and you will understand the difference between taste and flavor. You've probably noticed before that flavor is similarly impoverished when you have a stuffy nose.

> **retronasal olfactory sensation** The sensation of an odor that is perceived when chewing and swallowing force an odorant in the mouth up behind the palate into the nose. Such odor sensations are perceived as originating from the mouth, even though the actual contact of odorant and receptor occurs at the olfactory mucosa flavor The combination of true taste (sweet, salty, sour, bitter) and retronasal olfaction.
>
> **flavor** The combination of true taste (sweet, salty, sour, bitter) and retronasal olfaction.

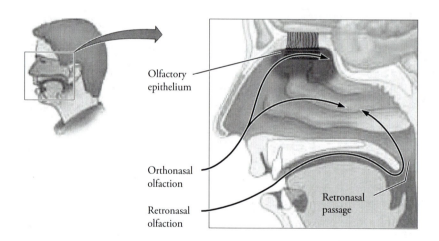

FIGURE 14.1. *Molecules released into the air inside our mouths as we chew and swallow food travel up through the retronasal passage into the nose, where they then move upward and contact the olfactory epithelium.*

Foods are also perceived by the somatosensory system via touch, temperature, and pain receptors in the tongue and mouth. Some of these sensations have protective functions: the burn of acid (which might damage your stomach if swallowed), the heat pain from scalding coffee, the pain of biting the tongue, and so on. Somatosensations also provide information about the nature of foods and beverages. For example, we get information about the fat content of foods from tactile sensations such as oily, viscous, thick, and creamy.

Localizing Flavor Sensations

You should have realized something else when you performed the chocolate experiment described in the previous section: even though you now know that the chocolate sensation originates from the olfactory receptors in your nose, you probably still perceived the flavor as coming entirely from your mouth. This perception is due in part to the tactile sensations evoked by chewing and swallowing, and in part to taste. Because you taste and feel the food only in your mouth (not in your nose), your brain concludes that the sensations must have arisen entirely from the mouth. Exceptions include foods such as horseradish, wasabi, and spicy mustard, which give off volatile chemicals that activate pain receptors all the way up through the retronasal passage. But these exceptions prove the rule: when we eat these foods, we experience the sensations as coming from our noses as well as our mouths.

Now consider the following curious case. A patient with normal olfaction but damaged taste and oral touch reported that she could smell lasagna, but when she ate it, it had no flavor. A similar effect was produced in a laboratory using a small amount of lidocaine and a large amount of blueberry yogurt. Subjects in this study had their left **chorda tympani** (one of the **cranial nerves** that carries information from taste receptors to the brain) anesthetized with the lidocaine while they tasted the yogurt. In this situation, the subjects reported that the blueberry sensation—which is entirely due to retronasal olfaction—seemed to come only from the right side of the mouth. Moreover, the intensity of the blueberry sensation was reduced, and this intensity was reduced even further when both taste nerves were blocked (D. J. Snyder et al. 2001).

In both the patient and the experimental subjects, the pathway from the mouth to the nasal cavity was completely intact. Why, then, were their retro-nasal lasagna and blueberry sensations reduced? Recent brain-imaging research by Dana Small appears to answer this question: the brain processes odors differently, depending on whether they come from the mouth or through the nostrils. This distinction makes good sense functionally because the significance of odors in the mouth is very different from that of odors sniffed from the outside world.

chorda tympani The branch of cranial nerve VII (the facial nerve) that carries taste information from the anterior, mobile tongue (the part that can be stuck out). The chorda tympani nerve leaves the tongue with the lingual branch of the trigeminal nerve (cranial nerve V) and then passes through the middle ear on its way to the brain.

cranial nerves Twelve pairs of nerves (one from each pair for each side of the body) that originate in the brain stem and reach sense organs and muscles through openings in the skull.

Without the proper cues to tell us where an odorant is coming from, input from the olfactory receptors apparently cannot be routed to the proper brain area to connect the smell sensation with the food stimulus.

The connections between taste and smell have been understood by the food industry for many years (Noble 1996). For example, if a company is marketing pear juice and wants to intensify the sensation of pear, it will add sugar. The increase in sweetness (a pure taste sensation) will increase the perceived olfactory sensation of pear. However, this will work only for pairs of taste and retronasal olfaction that are commonly experienced. If our pear juice company were to add salt, the pear sensation would not increase. Thus, learning plays a role in this phenomenon.

The pervasiveness of food additives such as carrageenan, guar gum, and other thickening agents shows that the food industry also has a good handle on the effects of somatosensation on food perception. And the ingredient lists of most processed foods include at least one artificial coloring, testifying to the importance of yet another sense, vision, in how we perceive foods.

ANATOMY AND PHYSIOLOGY OF THE GUSTATORY SYSTEM

Taste perception consists of the following sequence of events (the structures involved are illustrated in **Figure 14.2**). Chewing breaks down food substances into molecules, which are dissolved in saliva. The saliva-borne food molecules flow into a taste pore that leads to the **taste buds** embedded in structures called **papillae** (singular *papilla*) that cover the tongue (if the olfactory epithelium is the retina of the nose, the tongue is the retina of the mouth). Each taste bud, in turn, contains a number of **taste receptor cells**. Each taste receptor cell responds to a limited number of molecule types; when one of its preferred molecules makes contact with it, it produces action potentials that send information along one of the cranial nerves to the brain.

taste buds Globular clusters of cells that have the function of creating the neural signals conveyed to the brain by taste nerves. Some of the cells in the taste bud have specialized sites on their apical projections that interact with taste stimuli. Some of the cells form synapses with taste nerve fibers.

papillae Structures that give the tongue its bumpy appearance. From smallest to largest, the papillae types that contain taste buds are fungiform, foliate, and circumvallate; filiform papillae, which do not contain taste buds, are the smallest and most numerous.

taste receptor cells Cells within the taste bud that contain sites on their apical projections that can interact with taste stimuli. These sites fall into two major categories: those interacting with charged particles (e.g. sodium and hydrogen ions), and those interacting with specific chemical structures.

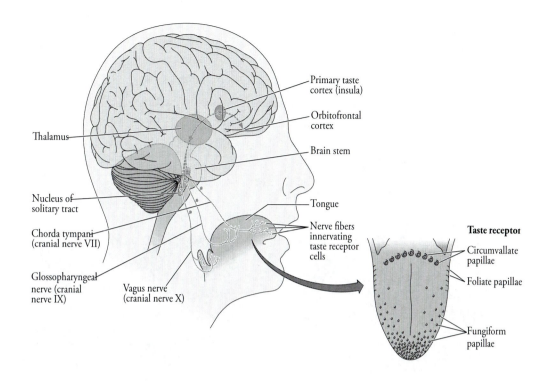

FIGURE 14.2. *The locations of each type of taste papilla are identified in the diagram of the tongue shown here. Neural signals from the taste buds in those papillae are transmitted via cranial nerves VII, IX, and X to the brain.*

Papillae

Papillae give the tongue its bumpy appearance and come in four major varieties, three of which contain taste buds.

Filiform papillae, the ones *without* any taste function, are located on the anterior portion of the tongue (the part we stick out when giving someone a raspberry) and come in different shapes in different species. In cats, they are shaped like tiny spoons with sharp edges. The filiform papillae on our tongues do not have these sharp edges, which is why you will find lapping milk from a bowl considerably more difficult than your cat does.

Fungiform papillae, so named because they resemble tiny button mushrooms, are also located on the anterior part of the tongue. They are visible to the naked eye, but blue food coloring swabbed onto the tongue makes them particularly easy to see (the blue food coloring stains the filiform papillae much better than the fungiform papillae, so the fungiform papillae appear as light circles against a darker

> **filiform papillae** Small structures on the tongue that provide most of the bumpy appearance. Filiform papillae have no taste function.

blue background). Fungiform papillae vary in diameter, but the maximum is about 1 millimeter. On average, about six taste buds are buried in the surface of each fungiform papilla. If we stain the tongues of many individuals, we see a large amount of variation (**Figure 14.3**). Some tongues have so few fungiform papillae that their stained tongues appear to have polka dots on them. Other tongues have so many that the polka dots are wall-to-wall.

> **fungiform papillae** Mushroom-shaped structures (maximum diameter 1 millimeter) that are distributed most densely on the edges of the tongue, especially the tip. Taste buds (an average of six per papilla) are buried in the surface.

(*a*) Nontaster

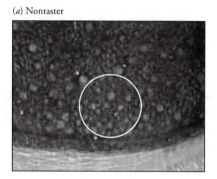

(*b*) Supertaster

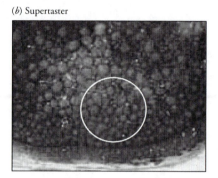

FIGURE 14.3. *Examples showing typical variability in density of fungiform papillae from one individual to the next. The circles (6 mm diameter) show a template used to provide counts of the number of fungiform papillae, which can then be compared across individuals (the circle is about the size of a hole made by a paper punch). In extreme cases, normal individuals may have as few as 5 fungiform papillae in that area or as many as 60.*

Foliate papillae are located on the sides of the tongue at the point where the tongue is attached. Under magnification, they look like a series of folds. Taste buds are buried in the folds.

Finally, **circumvallate papillae** are relatively large circular structures forming an inverted *V* on the rear of the tongue. These papillae look like tiny islands surrounded by moats. The taste buds are buried in the sides of the moats.

Although most people don't realize this, there are also taste buds on the roof of the mouth where the hard and soft palates meet. To demonstrate these, wet your finger and dip it into salt crystals. Touch the roof of your

> **foliate papillae** Folds of tissue containing taste buds. Foliate papillae are located on the rear of the tongue lateral to the circumvallate papillae, where the tongue attaches to the mouth.
>
> **circumvallate papillae** Circular structures that form an inverted *V* on the rear of the tongue (three to five on each side). Circumvallate papillae are moundlike structures surrounded by a trench (like a moat). These papillae are much larger than fungiform papillae.

mouth and move your finger back until you feel the bone end (the margin between the hard and soft palates). You will experience a flash of saltiness as you move the salt crystals onto the taste buds arrayed on that margin.

In sum, the taste buds are distributed in a line across the roof of the mouth and in papillae distributed in an oval on the tongue. Fungiform papillae make up the front of the oval, and foliate and circumvallate papillae make up its rear. Note that we have no subjective awareness of this distribution of taste buds.

Taste Buds and Taste Receptor Cells

Each taste bud is a cluster of elongated cells, organized much like the segments of an orange (**Figure 14.4**). The tips of some of the cells—the taste receptor cells—end in slender **microvilli** (singular *microvillus*) containing the sites that bind to taste substances. In an earlier era, these microvilli were mistakenly thought to be tiny hairs; we now know that microvilli are extensions of the cell membrane.

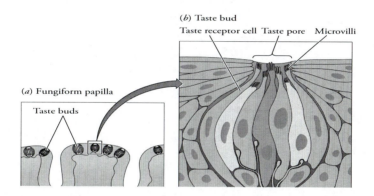

FIGURE 14.4. *Taste buds. (a) The location of the taste buds buried in the tissue on the tops of the fungiform papillae. (b) Cross section of a taste bud.*

Taste nerve fibers were once believed to be connected to receptors on one end and the brain at the other end. A considerably more complex series of events is now beginning to emerge. At least some receptors are on cells that do not synapse with taste nerve fibers; the information they convey must get to the nerve fibers in some other way (Herness et al. 2005; Roper 2006).

In fungiform papillae, the taste nerve fibers that enter the taste buds branch so that an individual cell can be innervated by more than one taste fiber and an individual taste fiber can innervate more than one cell. Taste receptors have a limited life span. After about 10 days they

> **microvilli** Slender projections on the tips of some taste bud cells that extend into the taste pore.

die and are replaced by new cells. This constant renewal enables the taste system to recover from a variety of sources of damage, and it explains why our taste systems remain robust even into old age. Recordings from taste nerve fibers show that different receptor cells contacted by branches of a single fiber show similar specificities to taste stimuli. In other words, it appears that the nerve fibers are somehow able to select the cells with which they will synapse so that the message they convey remains stable, even though the receptor cells are continually replaced.

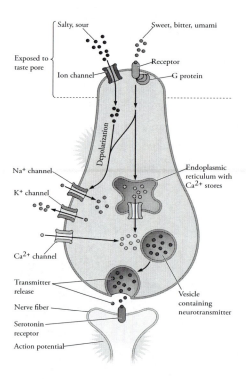

FIGURE 14.5. *Diagram of a taste receptor cell illustrating the different receptor mechanisms for ionic stimuli (salty and sour), as well as those using a lock-and-key mechanism (sweet, bitter, umami).*

The mechanisms that permit a taste cell to recognize a taste stimulus, known as a **tastant**, contacting its microvilli can be divided into two large categories (**Figure 14.5**). One class of tastants is made up of small, charged molecules that taste salty or sour. Small openings, called "ion channels," in microvilli membranes allow some types of charged particles to enter cells but bar others. When the charged particles in salty and sour foods enter salty and sour receptor cells, these cells signal their respective tastes.

Tastants in the second class, which produce sensations that we label as sweet or bitter, are perceived via a mechanism similar to that in the

| **tastant** Any stimulus that can be tasted. |

olfactory system, using G protein-coupled receptors (GPCRs). The GPCRs wind back and forth across microvillus membranes, and when a particular tastant molecule "key" is fitted into the "lock" portion of a GPCR on the outside of the membrane, the portion of the GPCR inside the cell starts a cascade of molecular events that eventually causes an action potential to be sent to the brain.

Taste Processing in the Central Nervous System

After leaving the taste buds through the cranial nerves, gustatory information travels through way stations in the medulla and thalamus before reaching the cortex (**Figure 14.6**) (Pritchard and Norgren 2004). The primary cortical processing area for taste—the part of the cortex that first receives taste information—is the **insular cortex**. The **orbitofrontal cortex** receives projections from the insular cortex. Some orbitofrontal neurons are multimodal. That is, they respond to temperature, touch, and smell, as well as to taste, suggesting that the orbitofrontal cortex may be an integration area.

Inhibition plays an important role in the processing of taste information in the brain. One of the functions of this inhibition may be to protect our whole-mouth perception of taste in the face of injuries to the taste system. Our brains receive taste input from several nerves (see **Figure 14.6**). Damage to one of them diminishes its contribution to the whole; however, that damage also releases the inhibition that is normally produced by the damaged nerve. The result is that whole-mouth taste intensities are relatively unchanged. Unfortunately, this preserved whole-mouth perception comes with a cost in some cases. Localized taste damage is often accompanied by "phantom taste" sensations (recall the phantom limbs experienced by many limb amputees, described in Chapter 12), as if the release of inhibition permits even noise in the nervous system to be perceived as a taste.

Descending inhibition from the taste cortex to a variety of other structures (DiLorenzo and Monroe 1995) may also serve other functions. For example, mouth injuries that lead to oral pain make it harder to eat. The inhibition of such pain perceptions by taste-processing parts of the brain would make eating easier and thus increase the likelihood of survival (because no matter how much the mouth hurts, we still have to eat). Consistent with this principle, patients with a serious oral pain disorder (burning mouth syndrome) were shown to have localized taste damage as well (Grushka and Bartoshuk 2000). Furthermore, women who have taste damage are more likely to suffer from severe nausea and vomiting during pregnancy (Sipiora et al. 2000), and cancer patients, whose chemotherapy and radiation therapy is known to damage the taste system, are more

insular cortex The primary cortical processing area for taste—the part of the cortex that first receives taste information.

orbitofrontal cortex The part of the frontal lobe of the cortex that lies above the bone (orbit) containing the eyes.

likely to experience coughing, gagging, and hiccups. In all these cases, inhibitory signals from the taste cortex that normally help prevent eating-disruptive symptoms (oral pain, vomiting, hiccuping, and so on) may have been turned off because of the damage to the taste system.

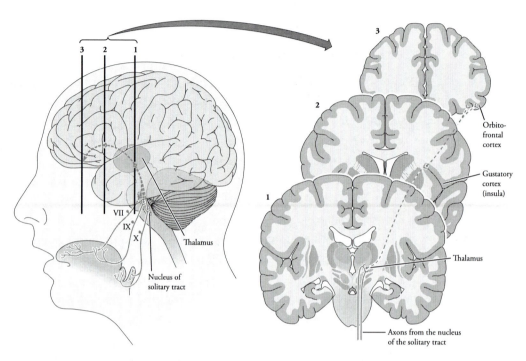

FIGURE 14.6. *Taste information projects from the tongue to the medulla, then to the thalamus (shown in cross section 1 of the brain), then to the insula (cross section 2), and finally to the orbitofrontal cortex (cross section 3).*

THE FOUR BASIC TASTES

We learned in the previous chapter that we are able to distinguish many different odorants. Already in this chapter, however, we have seen that when olfaction is taken out of the equation, much of the complexity of the sensations evoked by foods vanishes. Thus, we are led to believe that the number of basic taste qualities is quite small. In fact, the current universally accepted list includes only the four **basic tastes** previously mentioned in the section on taste buds and taste receptor cells: **salty, sour, bitter,** and **sweet**. As we discuss these in the sections that follow, note that one of the most important features of these basic tastes is that our liking (or disliking) for them is "hardwired" in the brain; that is, we are essentially born liking or disliking these tastes. This is very different from the way we learn to like or dislike odors.

Salty

Salts are made up of two charged particles: a cation (positively charged) and an anion (negatively charged). For example, common table salt is NaCl; the sodium is the cation (Na^+) and the chloride is the anion (Cl^-). Although all salts taste at least a little salty to humans, pure NaCl is the saltiest-tasting salt around. Sodium must be available in relatively large quantities to maintain nerve and muscle function, and loss of body sodium leads to a swift death.

Our ability to perceive saltiness is not static. Gary Beauchamp and his colleagues (Bertino, Beauchamp, and Engelman 1982) showed that diet can affect the perception of saltiness. Fortunately for those on low-sodium diets, reduced sodium intake increases the intensity of saltiness over time. Individuals who are initially successful in reducing their sodium intake will find that foods they used to love may now taste too salty. This adjustment in perception helps them keep their sodium intake down.

Our liking for saltiness is not static either. Early experiences can modify salt preference. In 1978 and 1979, several hundred infants were fed soy formulas that were accidentally deficient in chloride because of an error in formulation. Chloride deficiency has effects on our physiologies that mimic the effects of sodium deficiency. Thus, the infants who were chloride-deficient offered an important way to study sodium deficiency in humans. The Centers for Disease Control and Prevention in Atlanta monitored these infants, and a variety of studies were done to assess any potential damage. One of the consequences was that the salt preference of the children increased (L. J. Stein et al. 1996). Experiences during gestation can also affect salt preference. Crystal and Bernstein (1995) found an increased preference for salty snacks among college students whose mothers had experienced moderate to severe morning sickness during pregnancy. The exact mechanisms by which these abnormal metabolic events enhance salt preference are still not understood.

Sour

As you may remember from high school chemistry, a solution containing hydrogen ions (H^+) and hydroxide ions (OH^-) in equal proportions

---

basic tastes The four taste qualities that are generally agreed to describe human taste experience: sweet, salty, sour, bitter.

salty The taste quality produced by the cations of salts (e.g. the sodium in sodium chloride produces the salty taste). Some cations also produce other taste qualities (e.g. potassium tastes bitter as well as salty). The purest salty taste is produced by sodium chloride (NaCl), common table salt.

sour The taste quality produced by the hydrogen ion in acids.

bitter The taste quality, generally considered unpleasant, produced by substances like quinine or caffeine.

sweet The taste quality produced by some sugars, such as glucose, fructose, and sucrose. These three sugars are particularly biologically useful to us, and our sweet receptors are tuned to them. Some other compounds (e.g. saccharin, aspartame) are also sweet.

produces water (HOH, or H_2O). As the relative proportion of H^+ increases (decreasing the pH level), the solution becomes more *acidic*. Why do you need to be reminded of all this? Because sour is the taste of acids. Some individuals like the sourness of acids in relatively low concentrations. Many adults enjoy pickles and sauerkraut, both of which get their sour tastes from lactic acid, and the success of sour candies shows that many children like sour tastes that adults reject (Liem and Mennella 2003). At high concentrations, however, acids will damage both external and internal body tissues.

Bitter

The Human Genome Project revealed a multigene family responsible for about 25 different bitter receptors. The HUGO Gene Nomenclature Committee has established the rules for naming genes. (HUGO stands for Human Genome Organisation, an international organization of scientists involved in human genetic and genomic research.) The bitter gene family is *Tas2r* (*Tas#r* stands for taste, with the "2" indicating bitter—we will see below that a "1" indicates sweet); numbers following the *r* indicate the particular gene that is a member of that family. The bitter genes are located on three different chromosomes: 5, 7, and 12. Some of the bitter stimuli that excite each of the receptors expressed by these genes are now known. For example, a group of phytonutrients (compounds derived from edible plants) have been shown to stimulate taste receptors expressed by *Tas2r16*. One of these compounds, salicin, is an extract from willow bark that we know well as a compound related to aspirin (Bufe et al. 2002). But for most of the bitter stimuli we experience routinely, the receptors are still unknown.

Quinine (**Figure 14.7**), which is used to treat malaria, is one example of a bitter compound. Tonic water (which contains quinine), was originally formulated as a treatment for malaria (now, however, we know that unfortunately it does not contain enough quinine for that purpose). Tonic water does, however, contain enough quinine to taste very bitter, and for this reason lots of sugar was added to make the tonic water palatable. This approach works because sweet and bitter tastes inhibit one another; tonic water tastes much less bitter than the quinine content alone would and also tastes much less sweet than the sugar added alone would. Tonic water actually contains about the same amount of sugar as do other carbonated beverages

Each bitter receptor does not project via a specific bitter neuron. What this means is that, although a great many different compounds taste bitter, we generally do not distinguish between the tastes of these compounds (Mueller et al. 2005); we simply avoid them all. The diversity of receptors for bitterness enables species or even individuals in a given species to have varying responses to an array of bitter compounds. One of the most famous of these is "taste blindness" to PTC (phenylthiocarbamide) found in humans—a phenomenon we will revisit later in this chapter.

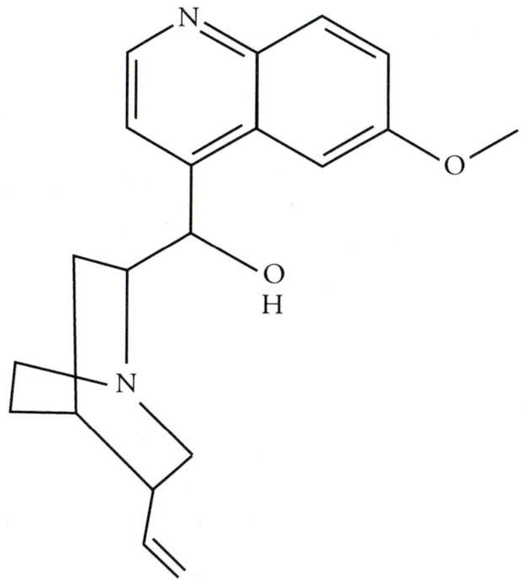

FIGURE 14.7. *The molecular structure of quinine ($C_{20}H_{24}N_2O_2$), a prototypically bitter substance.*

Not coincidentally, compounds that taste bitter to us tend to be poisonous. However, some bitter stimuli are actually good for us. For example, bitter compounds in some vegetables help protect against cancer. We would like to be able to "turn off" these bitter sensations to make it easier for people to eat their vegetables. Along these lines, Robert Margolskee, a pioneer in studies of bitter transduction, used his understanding of the bitter system to identify a substance that can inhibit some bitter sensations: adenosine monophosphate (AMP) (Ming, Ninomiya, and Margolskee 1999). AMP may actually function as a natural bitter inhibitor in mother's milk. A number of compounds in milk, such as casein (milk protein) and calcium salts, taste bitter; and, as we will see later, aversions to bitter tastes are present at birth. The presence of AMP in mother's milk may suppress those bitter tastes enough to allow milk to be palatable to babies who are particularly responsive to them.

Bitter perception is also affected by hormone levels in women. Sensitivity to bitterness intensifies during pregnancy and diminishes after menopause (Duffy et al. 1998). These differences make sense in the context of the function of bitterness as a poison detection mechanism. Intensifying the perception of bitter early in pregnancy, when toxins exert their maximum effects, has clear biological value. Consistent with this correlation, some of the aversions during pregnancy occur with foods or beverages that have bitter tastes (e.g. coffee).

Sweet

Sweetness is evoked by sugars, simple carbohydrates that generally conform to the chemical formula $(CH_2O)_n$, where n is between 3 and 7. Glucose, one of the sweetest-tasting sugars, is the principal source of energy in humans (as well as nearly every other living thing on Earth). Common table sugar, sucrose (**Figure 14.8**)—which is a combination of glucose and yet another sugar, fructose—tastes even sweeter.

The biological function of sweet is different from that of bitter, and the way taste receptors are tuned supports that biological difference. Many different molecules taste bitter. Our biological task is not to distinguish among them but rather to avoid them all. Thus, we have multiple bitter receptors to encompass the chemical diversity of poisons, but they all feed into a common line leading to rejection. With regard to sweet, some biologically useless sugars have structures very similar to those of glucose, fructose, and sucrose. In this case, then, the task of the taste system is to tune receptors so specifically that the biologically important sugars stimulate sweet taste but the others do not.

FIGURE 14.8. *The molecular structure of sucrose, common table sugar. This disaccharide is formed from a combination of a glucose molecule and a fructose molecule. Glucose, which is easily extracted from sucrose by the digestive system, is the main fuel that powers almost every biological engine (including the human brain currently reading this book).*

Consistent with the biological purpose of sweet, the family of genes expressing sweet receptors is very small: *Tas1r2* and *Tas1r3*. (We will discuss a third member of this family, *Tas1r1*, later). These genes express three different G protein-coupled receptors: T1R1, T1R2, and T1R3.

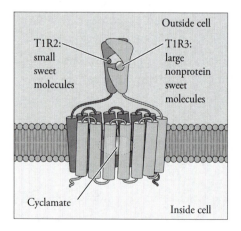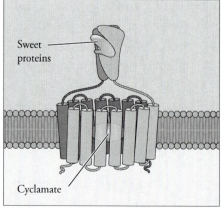

FIGURE 14.9. *Structure of the T1R2–T1R3 heterodimer sweet receptor, showing binding sites for both large and small sweet molecules. (After Temussi 2007.)*

Simple molecules (monomers) can form chains of varying length (polymers). When the chain has only two units, it is called a dimer; when the two units are different, it is called a heterodimer. Receptors T1R2 and T1R3 combine to form the heterodimer that is now thought to be the primary sweet receptor (**Figure 14.9**). The complex extracellular portion of this combination (which resembles the form of a Venus flytrap) provides a variety of positions at which sweeteners with very different chemical structures can bind. For example, sweet proteins are very large compared to smaller sweeteners like sucrose, and these sweet proteins can act like wedges that insert into the trap of the Venus flytrap domain and trigger the receptor. Smaller sweeteners (sugars, saccharin, aspartame, and so on) can interact with this same site or with other sites on the receptor.

The discovery that a single receptor is responsible for all sweet perception was very exciting to taste investigators, but it introduced a new sweetness puzzle. Different sweeteners stimulate different parts of the receptor, but whatever the source of stimulation is, the receptor produces the same signal. Therefore, all sweeteners—sugars and artificial sweeteners alike—would produce the same sweetness. However, artificial sweeteners like saccharin and aspartame do not taste exactly like sugar; if they did, there would be no need to continually search for better artificial sweeteners. Some claim that artificial sweeteners produce additional tastes that account for the difference. For example, saccharin tastes bitter as well as sweet to many. But some of us (the author included) do not taste the bitterness of saccharin at all; we are quite convinced that it is the nature of the sweetness that differs. Genetic studies may offer some help here. The receptor T1R3 appears to be able to function alone to respond only to high concentrations of sucrose (Zhao et al. 2003). This unique functionality could create the difference that many of us perceive between the sweetness of sucrose and that of artificial sweeteners.

Since our taste system can produce sweet receptors so precisely tuned to the biologically useful sugars, what is going on with artificial sweeteners? As far as we know, these sweeteners are biologically useful for only those interested in losing weight, but there is some doubt about whether even this is true.

Saccharin was discovered in 1879 when a research fellow working on coal tar derivatives failed to wash up before dinner and subsequently noticed that the tar residue on his hands tasted sweet. Another artificial sweetener was discovered in 1937, by a graduate student working in what must have been a messy lab. When he tasted sweet while smoking a cigarette, he realized that some compound in the lab must be responsible. In this way, cyclamate was discovered. Cyclamate was very popular for a few years, but suspicions were raised that it was carcinogenic. Although that suspicion was challenged and cyclamate remains legal in a number of other countries, the FDA (Food and Drug Administration) banned it in the United States. Artificial sweeteners are attractive to dieters because their sweet taste comes with essentially no calories. Countless dieters count on this property to help them watch their weight, but a 1986 epidemiological study showed that women who consumed artificial sweeteners actually gained weight (Stellman and Garfinkel 1986).

That same year, John Blundell, an English expert on weight regulation, published a provocative article suggesting that aspartame (the artificial sweetener sold as NutraSweet) increases appetite (Blundell and Hill 1986). Was the benefit of the reduced calories lost when individuals using aspartame actually increased their caloric intake in subsequent meals? T. L. Davidson and S. E. Swithers (2004) elaborated on this kind of thinking. They point to the fact that the "obesity epidemic" reflected in increasing weight in the American public occurred over the same years as the introduction of low-calorie foods into the American market. They argue that the uncoupling of the sensory properties of these diet foods from their metabolic consequences disrupts regulation, leading to weight gain.

Survival Value of Taste

Like olfactory receptors, taste receptors detect specific features of molecules. But the two associated senses evolved to serve quite different functions. The sense of smell helps us identify objects in our environment. Indeed, for many animals (e.g. rodents), olfaction is the primary means for knowing what surrounds them in the world. Consistent with this purpose, the olfactory system is capable of distinguishing a large number of different molecules, and an individual animal can learn about whatever olfactory stimuli exist in the environment where it happens to live.

On the other hand, we've just seen that the gustatory system responds to a fixed and much smaller set of molecules. This precise tuning is consistent with the role of taste as a system for detecting nutrients and "antinutrients" (substances that are either helpful or harmful, respectively, to our bodies) before we ingest them.

Each of the four basic tastes is responsible for a different nutrient or anti-nutrient, and has evolved according to its purpose. For example, the bitter taste subsystem is nature's poison detector. In terms of chemical structure, poisons are quite diverse. This diversity makes sense because any built-in poison detector must be able to recognize many different compounds. On the other hand, given that we don't really care if we can discriminate among poisons, since we just want to avoid them all, we could hook all of those receptors up to a few common lines to the brain. As we saw earlier, this is exactly how the bitter subsystem is set up.

Similarly, the sour subsystem is configured to reject any acidic solution without distinguishing exactly what is causing the acidity of the solution to be so high. The other two taste subsystems enable us to detect, and therefore selectively ingest, foods that our bodies need: sodium (salty) and sugars (sweet).

THE PLEASURES OF TASTE

Pfaffmann wrote a famous paper in 1960 entitled "The Pleasures of Sensation," in which he underlined unique features of the sense of taste with regard to affective experience. Taste provides not only sensory information about certain nutrients, but also pleasure (sweet, salty, and, for children, sour) and displeasure (bitter). The pleasure or displeasure that these tastes evoke is present at birth. That is, with no experience, an infant will like sweet and dislike bitter and strong sour. Salty receptors are not completely mature at birth, but when they do become functional, infants will like relatively dilute salts.

Some of the most impressive evidence for this hardwired affect with taste came from the work of Jacob Steiner on facial expressions in newborn infants (Steiner 1973). Steiner found that infants responded with stereotyped facial expressions when sweet, salty, sour, and bitter solutions were applied to their tongues. Sweet evoked a "smilelike" expression followed by sucking (**Figure 14.10***a*). Sour produced pursing and protrusion of the lips (**Figure 14.10***b*). Bitter produced gaping, movements of spitting, and in some cases, vomiting movements. Even infants born without cerebral hemispheres (a condition known as "anencephaly") showed the same facial expressions, suggesting that these expressions are mediated by very primitive parts of the brain.

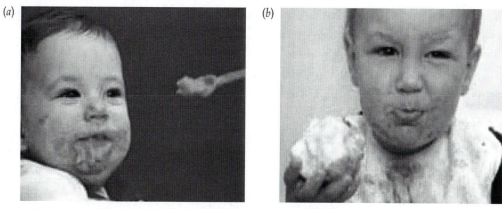

(a) (b)

FIGURE 14.10. *The two toddlers' facial expressions reveal the taste qualities that they are experiencing. (a) Sweet potato produces the typical smile associated with the acceptance of sweet. (b) Green apple produces the puckery face associated with sour.*

This hardwired affect responds to body need. For example, craving for salt was demonstrated by a dramatic case described in 1940. A 3½-year-old boy with an intense craving for salt died when his salt intake was restricted during a hospital stay. An autopsy revealed a tumor of his adrenal gland that had caused his body to lose sodium. His salt craving had enabled his body to retain enough sodium to keep him alive (Wilkins and Richter 1940).

The fact that the basic tastes provide both information and affective experience enables organisms to solve critical nutritional problems immediately, without having to learn (which takes time). The newborn baby can nurse because the sweet taste of mother's milk is pleasurable. The baby can also reject poisons because the bitter tastes they evoke are aversive. The athlete who sweats or the new mother who loses blood can replace lost sodium because of the pleasant taste of salt.

Specific Hungers

Early on, Curt Richter proposed a simple mechanism for the regulation of nutrients: the **specific hungers theory**. According to this view, the need for a nutrient causes the body to crave it. Ingestion of the nutrient reduces the craving and brings the body back into balance. The case of the boy with the salt craving described in the previous section provided support for this theory. Another source of support was a treatment for schizophrenia that was popular in the 1940s. At the time, some experts believed that the brain, which depends on glucose for fuel, could be forcibly rested if blood glucose were driven to very low values with insulin. Intense cravings for sweet were an unexpected by-product of the therapy. Later laboratory studies confirmed that insulin injections produce increased liking for sweet.

Even more support for the idea of specific hungers seemed to come from the work of a pediatrician, Clara Davis. She allowed a group of 6-month-old infants to eat whatever they liked, to see if they would choose wisely (C. M. Davis 1928). The infants thrived, leading Davis to conclude that, when allowed to choose among a variety of healthy foods, infants had the ability to select a healthy diet.

The success of the specific hungers theory spurred further investigations that ultimately proved that the theory was limited only to sweet and salty. In one of the early studies, rats were fed a diet deficient in vitamin B_{12}, which made them sick. When the rats were offered a choice of remaining on the same diet or switching to a diet containing B_{12}, they immediately switched. But Paul Rozin conducted a crucial control. He gave the control rats the choice of the original diet or a different diet that was also deficient in B_{12}. These rats also immediately switched to the different diet. Thus, the rats in the original study were not specifically seeking B_{12}; they had simply learned to avoid the diet that made them ill (Rozin 1967).

Rozin's work ended belief in specific hungers as an explanation of dietary regulation for anything beyond sugar and salt. In retrospect, we can see that the theory lacked an important ingredient. For craving to cause an animal to seek out and take in a needed nutrient, a sensory cue would have to be unambiguously associated with the nutrient. The saltiness of salt and the sweetness of sugar could serve as such cues, but the B_{12} molecule does not produce a detectable cue in food (**Figure 14.11**).

> **specific hungers theory** The idea that deficiency of a given nutrient produces craving (a specific hunger) for that nutrient. Curt Richter first proposed this idea and demonstrated that cravings for salty or for sweet are associated with deficiencies in those substances. However, the idea proved wrong for other nutrients (e.g. vitamins).

FIGURE 14.11. *In our evolutionary past, when food was scarce and we had to expend considerable physical effort to get it, specific hungers for sugar and salt were adaptive. In the current era, in which foods are plentiful and easily obtained, these specific hungers (combined with the profit motive for the food industry) lead many to consume too much junk food. The nutrients in vegetables are, alas, largely undetectable, so we cannot develop specific hungers for them.*

We were left with a problem, though. How did Clara Davis's infants know how to select a healthy diet if specific hungers do not operate for all nutrients? It turned out that they were not selecting a healthy diet at all. They were simply eating a variety of the foods presented because they got bored eating single foods. Because all of the choices were healthy, all the infants needed to do was eat a variety. In the modern world, eating whatever we like will not produce good health, because too many of the available foods are not healthy. In fact, the specific hungers that are genuine can do us considerable harm; just think about our love for sweet and salty junk foods.

If specific hungers don't control all of what we eat, what does? Our likes and dislikes of food depend very much on our likes and dislikes of the retronasal olfactory sensations associated with foods. As we saw in the previous chapter, these olfactory likes and dislikes are not hardwired as those for taste are. Thus, our

umami The taste sensation evoked by monosodium glutamate.

monosodium glutamate (MSG) The sodium salt of glutamic acid (an amino acid).

affect toward foods is made up of the hardwired affect contributed by taste, combined with the learned affect contributed by retronasal smell.

The gastrointestinal tract (commonly referred to as the gut) plays a crucial role in this learning. The macronutrients (nutrients that provide calories) are carbohydrates (long chains of sugar molecules), proteins (chains of amino acids), and fats (chains of fatty acids attached to glycerol). Except for the special case of sugar (a very short chain), these macronutrient molecules are too large to be sensed by taste or olfactory receptors. When foods containing these macronutrients enter the gut, however, the macronutrients are broken into their constituent pieces. These pieces stimulate chemoreceptors in the gut, and the brain makes us like the sensory properties (primarily the retronasal olfactory sensations) of the foods (conditioned food preferences). On the other hand, if we experience nausea after eating, the brain makes us dislike the sensory properties of the foods (conditioned food aversions). Thus, we regulate our intake through a combination of hardwired basic tastes and learned responses to food flavors.

The Special Case of Umami

Umami arose as a candidate for a fifth basic taste as part of advertising claims by manufacturers of **monosodium glutamate (MSG)**, the sodium salt of glutamic acid. Identified by Japanese chemists in the early 1900s, MSG was initially marketed as a flavor enhancer, said to suppress unpleasant tastes and enhance pleasant ones. When taste experts proved skeptical, MSG manufacturers went on to claim that MSG was a fifth basic taste, speculating that it signaled protein and thus played an important role in nutrition. However, the umami taste is not perceptible in many foods containing proteins. Another reason why umami is an unlikely candidate for a fifth basic taste is that some individuals like it but others do not. Basic tastes signal nutrients with hardwired affect, so if umami were a basic taste, the vast majority of people would react to it in the same way.

Because glutamate is an important neurotransmitter, receptors for the molecule are common throughout the body. The argument that such receptors might have been harnessed by the taste system to signal umami gained respectability when neuroscientists Nirupa Chaudhari and Steve Roper identified a version of a glutamate receptor in rat taste papillae (Chaudhari, Landin, and Roper 2000). The glutamate receptor is linked to the sweet receptors. Sweet compounds stimulate the heterodimer made up of T1R2 and T1R3; umami stimulates another heterodimer, made up of T1R1 and T1R3.

Of special interest, Robert Margolskee (also a pioneer in the study of the sweet receptor) recently discovered that many taste receptors, including the glutamate receptor, are found in the gut. This exciting discovery suggests a different function for umami. Protein molecules are too large to be sensed by taste or smell, but proteins are made up of amino acids, including glutamic acid. When eaten, proteins are broken down into their constituent amino acids, providing stimuli for the glutamate receptors in the gut. These receptors can signal the brain that protein has been consumed. In this way, glutamate receptors can fulfill the function attributed to umami, but this is done in the gut, not the mouth. Consistent with this finding, John Prescott (a cognitive psychologist who studies the chemical senses) showed that consumption of a novel-flavored soup with MSG added to it produces a conditioned preference for the novel flavor. Simply holding the soup in the mouth does not (Prescott 2004).

Because glutamate is a neurotransmitter, concerns have been raised about its safety in the human diet. MSG became particularly notorious in the 1960s. First it became associated with Chinese restaurant syndrome—a constellation of symptoms including numbness, headache, flushing, tingling, sweating, and tightness in the chest—that was reported by some individuals after consuming MSG (Kwok 1968). Then Dr. John Olney, a toxicologist, suggested that MSG might induce brain lesions, particularly in infants (Olney and Sharpe 1969). In response to these concerns, MSG was removed from baby foods in the 1970s. The final conclusion as of now (see Walker and Lupien 2000) is that MSG in large doses may be a problem for some sensitive individuals, but apparently does not present a serious problem for the general population. For those who are sensitive, however, MSG can pose a serious risk.

The Special Case of Fat

Like protein, fat is a very important nutrient. Also like protein, fat molecules are too large to stimulate either taste or olfaction but are broken into their constituent parts by digestion in the gut. Fat molecules are made up of fatty acids attached to a support structure. Whole fat molecules stimulate the trigeminal nerve in the mouth, evoking tactile sensations like oily, viscous, creamy, and so on; but some fat molecules may be partially digested while still in the mouth, thus releasing fatty acids. Neurobiologist Tim Gilbertson's discovery of fatty acid receptors on the tongues of rats led to the idea that stimulation of these fatty acid receptors might play a hardwired role in our love of fat. Just as with glutamate, however, nature uses a more general method to ensure that we love fat-containing foods. Anthony Sclafani (a learning theorist who is an expert on conditioned food preferences) showed that fat in the gut produces conditioned preferences for the sensory properties of the food containing fat.

Once we understand the role of conditioning in food preferences, we should have a healthy skepticism about the value of so-called diet foods. Mimicking the sensory properties of normal foods but reducing the caloric content disrupts normal regulatory mechanisms, as noted by Davidson and Swithers (see the discussion of sweet earlier in this chapter).

> **labeled lines** A theory of taste coding in which each taste nerve fiber carries a particular taste quality. For example, the quality evoked from a sucrose-best fiber is sweet, that from an NaCl-best fiber is salty, and so on.

A major source of historical controversy in the taste literature revolved around whether tastes are coded mainly via **labeled lines**, in which each taste neuron would unambiguously signal the presence of a certain basic taste, or via patterns of activity across many different taste neurons. We've seen examples of both types of coding in other senses. For example, color vision and olfaction use pattern coding. A single type of cone cannot tell us the wavelength of a light ray, but the pattern of activity across our three cone types can give us this information. Hearing, on the other hand, uses a mechanism more akin to the labeled-line approach: certain neurons always respond best to 5000-Hz tones, others always respond best to 5100-Hz tones, and so on. Which scheme is used in the gustatory system?

Given what we've already learned about the functions of the four basic tastes, it is easy to construct an evolutionary argument for labeled-line coding. Recall that in olfaction, which uses pattern coding, mixtures of two different compounds very often produce a third smell sensation that bears no resemblance to the smells of the mixture components. Such a coding system would be disastrous for the purpose of the taste system. For example, poisonous plants contain components with a variety of tastes. If bitterness were to synthesize with these other tastes, we would not be able to parse it out and thus avoid the poison. The functions of the four tastes are well served by their independence from each other. In addition, studies have shown that we are, in fact, very good at analyzing taste mixtures. For example, tonic water, which contains a combination of quinine and sugar, tastes bittersweet: we have no difficulty identifying its two components—bitter and sweet.

The historical controversy arose because initial research seemed to indicate that most neurons coming from taste buds respond to more than one of the four basic tastes. In Carl Pfaffmann's classic work recording from single cat chorda tympani fibers, these fibers were not specific to the four basic tastes. For example, some fibers responded to both acid and salt, and others responded to both acid and quinine (Pfaffmann 1941). How could such a system code sour, salt, and bitter without confusion? Subsequent research showed that although "pure" labeled lines from individual receptor types are rare, most taste nerve fibers do have a clear "favorite" stimulus. Marion Frank (1973) named the fiber types "NaCl-best," "sucrose-best," and so on.

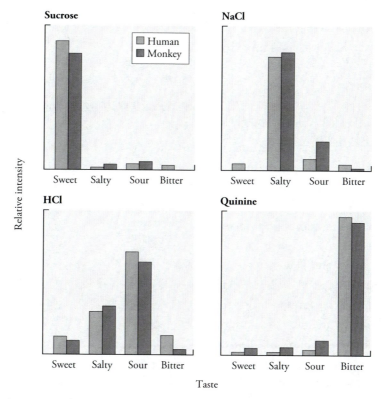

FIGURE 14.12. *The tastes that human subjects perceive for each of four stimuli: sucrose, NaCl, HCl, and quinine. Also shown are the tastes that a monkey would perceive if the monkey's sweet-best fibers coded sweetness, NaCl-best fibers coded saltiness, HCl-best fibers coded sourness, and quinine-best fibers coded bitterness. (Monkey data from Sato, Ogawa, and Yamashita 1975.)*

The fact that taste nerve fibers are not exclusively tuned to single basic tastes means that we rarely, if ever, experience "pure tastes." For example, sour tastes are perceived when acid-best fibers are activated, but acids also activate NaCl-best fibers (**Figure 14.12**). Thus, a solution of hydrochloric acid (HCl) will taste primarily sour, but also salty.

Taste Adaptation and Cross-Adaptation

As we've seen throughout this book, all sensory systems show adaptation effects, in which constant application of a certain stimulus temporarily weakens subsequent perception of that stimulus. In taste, our constant adaptation to the salt in saliva affects our ability to taste salt; in addition, adaptation to certain components in one food can change the perception of a second food.

You've experienced cross-adaptation yourself if you've ever noticed that a beverage like lemonade tastes too sour after you eat a sweet dessert. The sugar in the dessert adapts the sweet receptors so that the subsequent lemonade tastes less sweet and more sour than normal.

GENETIC VARIATION IN TASTE EXPERIENCE

In 1931 a chemist named Arthur Fox discovered that we do not all live in the same taste worlds (A. L. Fox 1931). Fox was synthesizing the compound phenylthiocarbamide (PTC) (**Figure 14.13***a*),

nontaster of PTC/PROP An individual born with two recessive alleles for the *Tas2r38* gene and unable to taste the compounds phenylthiocarbamide or propylthiouracil.

taster of PTC/PROP An individual born with one or both dominant alleles for the *Tas2r38* gene and able to taste the compounds phenylthiocarbamide and propylthiouracil. Tasters of PTC/PROP who also have a high density of fungiform papillae are supertasters.

when some spilled and flew into the air. A colleague nearby noticed a bitter taste, but Fox tasted nothing. A test of additional colleagues revealed a few more **nontasters** like Fox who did not taste the compound, but most (**tasters**) perceived it as bitter. The next year Albert Blakeslee (a famous geneticist of the day) and Fox took PTC crystals to a meeting of the American Association for the Advancement of Science and set up a voting booth for attendees to register their perceptions. About one-third of those polled found the crystals to be tasteless, while two-thirds found them to be bitter. These proportions captured the imagination of many researchers, and for several years the Journal of Heredity sold papers impregnated with PTC for further studies. Family studies eventually confirmed that taster status was an inherited trait (e.g. the Dionne quintuplets were all found to be tasters in 1941). Nontasters carried two recessive alleles, whereas tasters had either one or both dominant alleles.

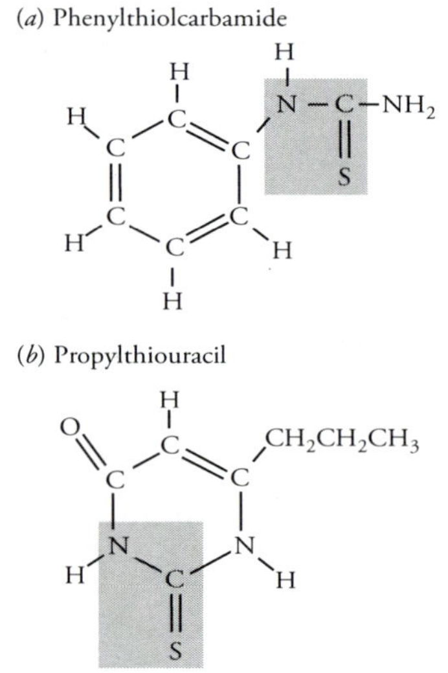

FIGURE 14.13. *The chemical structures of PTC (a) and PROP (b). The portions shaded in blue are those responsible for the bitter taste.*

Initially, individuals were simply classified according to whether they could taste PTC, but eventually threshold studies came into vogue. In a threshold method invented specifically for PTC studies, subjects were given eight cups, four containing water and four containing a given concentration of PTC. Correct sorting determined the threshold. The distribution of thresholds was bimodal, with nontasters showing very high thresholds and tasters showing low thresholds. This distribution varied by sex and race: women had lower thresholds than men, and Asians had lower thresholds than Caucasians.

In the 1960s, Roland Fischer shifted tests to a chemical relative of PTC that was safer to test—propylthiouracil (PROP) (**Figure 14.13***b*)—and focused on the nutritional implications of the genetic variation in taster status (Fischer and Griffin 1964). Fischer suggested that tasters were more finicky eaters: because bitter tastes are more intense to these individuals, they tend to dislike foods high in bitter compounds, such as many vegetables, that nontasters find more palatable. Fischer also related taster status to body type (e.g. weight) and health. Alcoholics and smokers were found to contain a lower proportion of tasters than would be expected by chance, presumably because unpleasant sensations (e.g. bitterness) produced by alcoholic beverages and tobacco acted as deterrents. The effect of genetic variation in taste was even related to cancer risk, as will be described shortly.

In 2003, Dennis Drayna and his colleagues discovered the location of the gene that expresses PTC/PROP receptors (Kim et al. 2003). This gene is a member of the bitter family introduced earlier and is designated *Tas2r38*. Individuals with two recessive alleles are nontasters; those with either one or both dominant alleles are tasters.

Supertasters

By the 1970s, the "direct" psychophysical methods introduced by Harvard's S. S. Stevens led to a new look at genetic variation in taste. Instead of measuring thresholds—the dimmest sensations—investigators could look at suprathreshold taste and plot the psychophysical functions showing how perceived taste intensity varies with concentration. Stevens and his students showed that the same relation held for many different sensory modalities, including taste:

$$\psi = \varphi^\beta$$

cross-modality matching The ability to match the intensities of sensations that come from different sensory modalities. This ability enables insight into sensory differences. To the average nontaster of PTC/PROP, for example, the bitterness of black coffee roughly matches the pain of a mild headache; for a supertaster, the bitterness of black coffee roughly matches the pain of a severe headache.

supertaster An individual who perceives the most intense taste sensations. A variety of factors may contribute to this heightened perception; among the most important is the density of fungiform papillae.

where ψ is perceived intensity, ϕ is concentration, and β takes on different values for different sensory modalities (S. S. Stevens and Galanter 1957). Of special interest for the present purposes, β takes on different values for different taste qualities. For example, bitterness grows more slowly with concentration than sweet does (**Figure 14.14**). That is, the value of β for bitter is smaller than the value of β for sweet.

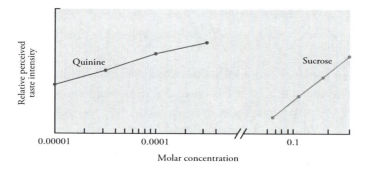

FIGURE 14.14. *Psychophysical functions for quinine and sucrose. The logarithm of the perceived taste intensity is plotted against the logarithm of the concentration. In this plot, β is the slope of the function. The value of β for quinine is 0.3; for sucrose, 0.8. (Data from Bartoshuk 1979.)*

Two of S. S. Stevens's students—Joseph Stevens and Lawrence Marks—made another fundamental discovery in this era: humans are very good at **cross-modality matching** (J. C. Stevens 1959). For example, we can match the loudness of a sound to the brightness of a light, and we can match both of these to the intensity of a taste. This finding led to yet another way to study variability in individuals' perceptions of the bitter taste of PTC and PROP (Marks et al. 1988): we could ask subjects to match the bitterness of PROP to other sensations completely unrelated to taste (**Figure 14.15**). For example, nontasters matched the taste of PROP to very weak sensations (the sound of a watch or a whisper). Tasters proved to be a heterogeneous lot. For some, PROP was likened to very intense sensations, such as the brightness of the sun or the most intense pain ever experienced. These individuals were labeled **supertasters**. "Medium tasters" matched PROP to weaker stimuli, such as the smell of frying bacon or the pain of a mild headache (Bartoshuk, Fast, and Snyder 2005).

Armed with genotypes, ratings of the bitterness of PROP, and counts of fungiform papillae, Valerie Duffy (a pioneer in the modern movement among nutritionists to evaluate food behavior in terms of the sensory properties of foods instead of only their nutrient content), along with her student John Hayes and colleagues (Hayes et al. 2008), was able to show that a combination of PROP genotype and tongue anatomy divided individuals into the three groups already described: nontasters, tasters, and supertasters. This research showed that PROP status and number of fungiform papillae are independent. The combination of ability to taste PROP and possession of a very large number of fungiform papillae produces a PROP supertaster; PROP tasters with fewer fungiform papillae are medium PROP tasters. PROP nontasters show the whole range of number of fungiform papillae. Thus, a person can be a PROP nontaster but be a supertaster in all other ways.

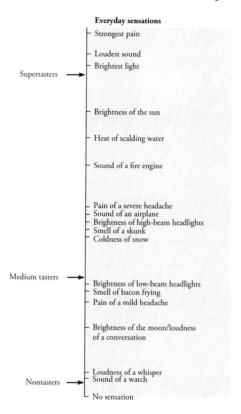

FIGURE 14.15. *Cross-modality matching. The levels of bitterness of concentrated PROP perceived by nontasters, medium tasters, and supertasters of PROP are shown on the left. The perceived intensities of a variety of everyday sensations are shown on the right. (Data from Fast 2004.)*

Those with the most fungiform papillae not only experience the most intense taste sensations in general, but also experience the most intense sensations of oral burn (e.g. chilis) and oral touch (fats, thickeners in foods) because fungiform papillae are innervated by nerve fibers that convey burn and touch sensations, as well as those that convey taste sensations. In addition, because of central connections between taste and retronasal olfaction, those who experience the most intense taste sensations also perceive more intense retronasal olfaction and thus more intense flavor.

Pathology adds yet another source of variation in our oral sensations. Surprisingly, removing input from one of the taste nerves (by anesthesia or damage) can actually intensify taste sensations (e.g. Lehman et al. 1995). This intensification results because inputs from the different taste nerves inhibit one another in the brain. Loss of input from one nerve releases others from that inhibition. In some cases, the result is actual intensification of whole-mouth taste.

Although the concept of supertasters originated because of studies on PROP bitterness, we now understand that a variety of factors contribute to the intensities of oral sensations. Thus, supertasters are best defined simply as those who experience the most intense taste sensations, but we add a note of caution: given the many sources of variation, we find ourselves with different types of supertasters.

Health Consequences of Taste Sensation

With these new insights, the potential links between responsiveness to PROP and health have become the focus of renewed interest. The new psychophysical methods permitted Valerie Duffy to show that variation in the sensory properties of foods and beverages affects food preferences and thus diet. Because diet is a major risk factor for a variety of diseases, genetic variation in taste plays a role in these diseases. For instance, some vegetables produce unpleasant sensations (e.g. bitter) to medium tasters and supertasters, leading these individuals to eat fewer of them. Reduced vegetable intake is in turn a risk factor for colon cancer.

Sure enough, Duffy and her colleagues found that, in a sample of older men getting routine colonoscopies at a Department of Veterans Affairs hospital, those tasting PROP as most bitter had the most colon polyps, a precursor to colon cancer (Basson et al. 2005). On the other hand, fats can produce unpleasantly intense sensations to supertasters, leading them to eat fewer high-fat foods and thereby lowering their risk of cardiovascular disease (Duffy, Lucchina, and Bartoshuk 2004). These sensory links to behavior that affects health are not limited to diet. Fischer's early suggestion that non-tasters are more likely to smoke and consume alcohol has proved correct (Duffy et al. 2004; D. J. Snyder et al. 2005).

Pleasure and Retronasal versus Orthonasal Olfaction

There is still much that is not understood about the links between retronasal and orthonasal (through the nostrils) olfaction, including the pleasure or displeasure associated with these sensations. We know that we learn to like or dislike smells, but do we learn these preferences separately for retro- and orthonasal olfaction? David Laing, an Australian expert on the chemical senses, suggested that this may be the case. He noted that many of us like the smell of recently cut grass, but few would like such a sensation if it turned up in food. On the other hand, when an aversion is learned retronasally, it often shows up with orthonasal olfaction as well. Bartoshuk recounts getting carsick on a childhood vacation while simultaneously eating chocolate-covered cherries. She now not only avoids the cherries, but finds cherry-scented soaps disgusting as well.

Chili Peppers

The pleasure that some people experience from chili peppers deserves special attention. We are not born liking chili peppers. Rozin studied the acquisition of chili pepper preference in Mexico and found that the process depended on social influences. Chili is gradually added to the diet of young children beginning at about age 3, and the children observe their family members enjoying it. By age 5 or 6, children voluntarily add chili to their own food. At some point the chili is liked for its own sake.

FIGURE 14.16. *Do these images inspire fear or delight in your taste buds?*

A variety of arguments based on presumed health benefits have been introduced to account for our love of chili peppers. For example, some have argued that chilis kill microorganisms in food, thus acting as a preservative. Others have argued that chilis contain vitamins A and C, which give them adaptive value (in other words, the pain of the chili serves as a cue for the presence of the vitamins). The pleasure that some people experience from chilis has also been linked to the idea that the resulting burn leads to the release of endorphins, the brain's internal painkillers.

One of the most interesting features of the liking for the burn of chili peppers is its near total restriction to humans. Rozin has documented a few cases on record of animals showing a liking for chilis, but in all cases these were pets fed chili pepper by their human companions. When Rozin tried to produce liking for chilis in rats, he failed. But one of Rozins students, Bennett Galef, who is famous for the study of social interactions among rats, was finally able to get rats to like a diet seasoned with a mild level of cayenne pepper by exposing the rats to a "demonstrator" rat that had just eaten the diet. It seems that growing to like chili peppers is a social phenomenon for rats as well.

The burn that we experience from chili peppers is highly variable across individuals (**Figure 14.16**). The variability comes from two sources. First, as noted earlier, individuals with the most fungiform papillae (supertasters) have the most fibers mediating pain, and thus they perceive the most intense oral burn from chilis. Second, capsaicin, the chemical that produces the burn in chilis, desensitizes pain receptors. This means that individuals who consume chilis quite often (once every 48 hours is sufficient) are chronically desensitized. Chili peppers produce considerably less burn to those who are desensitized.

Desensitization can come to your rescue if you accidentally order a meal that proves to be overspiced for your palate. After the first mouthful, wait until the burn has subsided. The mistake many diners make is to keep trying to eat. As long as the capsaicin continues to be applied, desensitization does not occur. Desensitization occurs during the decline of the burn (B. G. Green 1993). Once the initial burn has faded, the rest of the meal can be consumed with relative comfort.

Capsaicin desensitization has important clinical value. The ancient Mayan Indians used a concoction made of chilis to treat the pain of mouth sores. Wolffe Nadoolman, then a medical student at Yale working in Bartoshuk's laboratory, created a similar remedy by adding cayenne pepper to a recipe for taffy. Cancer patients often develop painful mouth sores from chemotherapy and radiation therapy, and if these patients suck on the capsaicin candies, capsaicin is brought into contact with the pain receptors stimulated by the sores. The pain receptors are then desensitized and the pain is dramatically reduced (Berger et al. 1995). Although capsaicin can be used to reduce pain at any body site, the skin is a potent barrier that prevents capsaicin from contacting pain receptors. Thus, capsaicin remedies for disorders like arthritis are rarely very satisfactory. In the mouth, the mucous membrane permits capsaicin to easily contact pain receptors, so there, desensitization is fast and powerful.

SUMMARY

1. Flavor is produced by the combination of taste and retronasal olfaction (olfactory sensations produced when odorants in the mouth are forced up behind the palate into the nose). Flavor sensations are localized to the mouth, even though the retronasal olfactory sensations come from the olfactory receptors high in the nasal cavity.

2. Taste buds are globular clusters of cells (like the segments in an orange). The tips of some of the cells (microvilli) contain sites that interact with taste molecules. Those sites fall into two groups: ion channels that mediate responses to salts and acids, and G protein-coupled receptors that bind to sweet and bitter compounds.

3. The tongue has a bumpy appearance because of structures called papillae. The filiform papillae (most numerous) have no taste buds. Taste buds are found in the fungiform papillae (front of the tongue), foliate papillae (rear edges of the tongue) and circumvallate papillae (rear center of the tongue), as well as on the roof of the mouth.

4. Taste projects ipsilaterally from the tongue to the medulla, thalamus, and cortex. It projects first to the insula in the cortex, and from there to the orbitofrontal cortex, an area where taste can be integrated with other sensory input (e.g. retronasal olfaction).

5. Taste and olfaction play very different roles in the perception of foods and beverages. Taste is the true nutritional sense; taste receptors are tuned to molecules that function as important nutrients. Bitter taste is a poison detection system. Sweet taste enables us to respond to the sugars that are biologically useful to us: sucrose, glucose, and fructose. Salty taste enables us to identify sodium, a mineral crucial to survival because of its role in nerve conduction and muscle function. Sour taste permits us to avoid acids in concentrations that might injure tissue.

6. Umami, the taste produced by monosodium glutamate, has been suggested as a fifth basic taste that detects protein. However, umami lacks one of the most important properties of a basic taste: hardwired affect. Some individuals like umami, but others do not. The presence of glutamate receptors in the gut suggests that protein detection occurs there. Digestion breaks down proteins into their constituent amino acids, and the glutamate released stimulates gut glutamate receptors, leading to conditioned preferences for the sensory properties of the foods containing the protein.

7. The importance of taste to survival requires that we be able to recognize each of the taste qualities, even when it is present in a mixture. By coding taste quality with labeled lines in much the same way that frequencies are coded in hearing, nature has ensured that we have this important capability. These labeled lines are noisy. For example, acids are able to stimulate fibers mediating saltiness, as well as those mediating sourness. Thus, acids tend to taste both salty and sour.

8. Foods do not taste the same to everyone. The Human Genome Project revealed that we carry about 25 genes for bitter taste. The most studied bitter receptor responds to PROP and shows allelic variation in humans leading to the designations, "nontaster" for those who taste the least bitterness and "taster" for those who taste the most. In addition, humans vary in the number of fungiform papillae (and thus taste buds) they possess. Those with the most taste buds are called supertasters and live in a "neon" taste world; those with the fewest live in a "pastel" taste world. Psychologists discovered these differences by testing people's ability to match sensory intensities of stimuli from different modalities. For example, the bitterness of black coffee matches the pain of a mild headache to nontasters but resembles a

severe headache to supertasters. The way foods taste affects palatability, which in turn affects diet. Poor diet contributes to diseases like cancer and cardiovascular disease.

9. For taste, unlike olfaction, liking and disliking are hardwired; for example, babies are born liking sweet and salty and disliking bitter. When we become deficient in salt or sucrose, liking for salty and sweet tastes, respectively, increases. Junk foods are constructed to appeal to these preferences. Liking the burn of chili peppers, on the other hand, is acquired and, with the exception of some pets, is essentially limited to humans. Because taste buds are surrounded by pain fibers, supertasters perceive much greater burn from chilis than do nontasters.

SALT
The Edible Rock

By Margaret Visser

In the earliest times, men usually let animals find salt for them. An outcrop of rock salt was called a salt-"lick" because animals went there to lick it. When the Europeans came to North America they did not find it trackless, for buffalo trails had been worn for centuries to the salt-licks, and it was along these smoothed shortcuts through and around natural obstacles that the first explorers began to move across the continent. Amazingly early in human history, men began to dig into the earth to find salt. All over the world, people like the Hallstatt miners have tunneled along salt seams, braving floods, the collapse of roofs and walls, exhaustion, salt-burn, suffocation, and accidents with their light-source, fire.

Modern salt-mining has become, in comparison, almost miraculously safe and productive. In many cases, mining engineers take advantage of what has always been considered one of the eeriest of the attributes of salt: the rock is not only edible but it also dissolves, and can be returned to its solid state again. Water is injected into the salt seams through tunnels bored from the surface; the brine is pumped out and then evaporated to produce salt again …

Another of salt's mysteries is this: if our bodies need so little, why do we crave it so much? Unlike the human "sweet tooth," our salt hunger is shared by animals: cows, for instance, love salt, and will lick a hole in a wall they find pleasantly salty. Our tongues are well supplied with salt-tasting buds, and to compound our frailty, saltiness enhances the taste of sweet things and disguises bitterness. It also helps make stale or spoiled food edible.

But many peoples have simply never known that salt existed and have lived perfectly healthy lives without it. Australian aborigines and American Indians and Inuit often knew no salt. Early human settlements were apparently not built to be near salt-springs. Human beings, it seems, learn about salt (and become addicted to it) at a very precise moment in their history: when they cease being almost exclusively carnivorous and learn to eat vegetables in quantities usually available only when they grow them themselves. When people begin not only to eat a lot of vegetables, but to reduce the salt content in their food by boiling it—a cooking method which presupposes the ability to make metal pots that can be set directly over a fire—then salt becomes more desirable still.

Carnivorous animals and meat-hunting men find enough salt in blood to satisfy them. Certain African tribes who have never been able to assure themselves of a salt supply, prick the necks of their living cattle and drink their blood. There is no immediate need to slaughter a cow for meat since, alive, she is a sort of walking larder, providing protein and salt.

It is herbivorous animals that love salt. One theory about the origin of the domestication of cattle by man is inspired by the "salt tie" which still operates between reindeer herders and their animals. Cattle may originally have been taught when very young that they could get their salt from men. They would then range freely in search of pasture. Their "owners" needed only to visit them occasionally in the field with gifts of salt to remind them that they were no longer wild. Men could then proceed to take advantage of the relationship.

Salt, in myths all over the world, is seen as a "newcomer," an addition whose necessity is not perceived before it arrives, but which is intensely attractive, indeed irresistible, once it is tried. Here, for example, is a North American Indian myth about the presence of a salt-lick near the home of the Indian who told it.

> Salt used to be far away. He was a man and was traveling through the country. The Indians never used salt then. He looked ugly all over, and the people did not like him. He came to a camp and said, "Let me put my hand in there, then the food will taste well."
>
> "No," said the cook, "I want to eat this, you look too ugly."
>
> He went off to another band and said, "Let me put my hand in here, and it will taste well."
>
> "No, your hand is too dirty."
>
> He came to another band and said the same thing, but people declined his offer. At last he came to a single man, and he was a cook. He said, "I want to put my hand into the food, then it will taste better." And the cook allowed him to do so, and he put in his hand.
>
> "Now taste it." The Indian tasted it and it was good. Salt settled there and stayed forever, about ten or twelve miles from St. Thomas.

Notice in this story that people are suspicious about salt. For one thing, eating it is eating earth, and that in itself is peculiar behavior. You add it to your food, it disappears, yet it indescribably alters the taste of everything you eat. Salt is weird, powerful, dangerous, and "extra." In religious symbolism it is always linked with "strong," powerful substances like iron or blood. We feel that a little of it is all we need, that this little has made all the difference, and that we ought not to abuse the privilege of having it. Furthermore, adding salt is being clever, and getting salt has always taxed human intelligence. By the same token we feel that we could easily be tricked by someone who cunningly adds salt without our knowing it, thus imparting a sinister attraction to something we ought not to want. When someone "salts" a mine he wishes to sell, he plants nuggets of gold in his worthless property for dupes to find …

Salt is both "farmed" like wheat, and "searched for" like game or wild berries. Bread (grown, harvested, ground, leavened, and baked) and salt (found, won, collected, and efficiently transported) together cover the field: they represent man as Farmer, patiently and wisely nurturing his crops, but also as Hunter, Scientist, Adventurer, and Organizer. Bread and salt are customarily offered in Russia (where the word for "hospitality" means literally "bread-salt") and in other countries, as a sign of welcome to a guest; bread and salt symbolize the precious stores of the house, the fruits of the host's labor, his patience, his ingenuity, his civilized foresight and preparedness.

Oath-taking, in many cultures, is a ceremony involving salt, just as the act of swearing may employ blood or iron as a sign denoting a person's unbreakable word. Salt is shared at table, in a context of order and contentment. Traditional Bedouin will never fight a man with whom they have once eaten salt. When the Lord God of Israel made a covenant with the Jews, it was a Covenant of Salt, denoting an unalterable bond of friendship. It also meant that the Jews had settled down in the Promised Land, had ceased to be sheepherding nomads, and would now eat the fruit of their harvests, cooked and seasoned with salt …

Salt is the only rock directly consumed by man. It corrodes but preserves, desiccates but is wrested from the water. It has fascinated man for thousands of years not only as a substance he prized and was willing to labor to obtain, but also as a generator of poetic and of mythic meaning. The contradictions it embodies only intensify its power and its links with experience of the sacred.

Salt brings flavor to life, and people accustomed to salt find their food tasteless, flat, and dull without it. This is the point of the folktale from which Shakespeare derived *King Lear*. In the original story, the younger daughter of the king, unlike her articulate and dishonest sisters, tells her father that her love for him is not like silver or gold, as they had claimed, but "like salt." Enraged, he throws her out of the palace. She eventually is to be married, and invites the king (who does not know who she is or recognize her under her veil) to the wedding feast. She has ordered all the food to be prepared without salt. The king, finding the dinner inedible, weeps for his youngest daughter and finally understands how important a pinch of humble salt is to man's happiness. She identifies herself, the two are reconciled—and presumably the saltcellars are produced with a flourish. The story shows that a daughter's sincere love is unassertive and may be taken for granted, but it is dependable and irreplaceable. In refusing or in losing it, a father is left without the kind of thing that gives zest to life.

When Jesus called his followers "the salt of the earth," he was telling them that they were irreplaceable, and that their mission was to give people what makes life worth living.

There were few of them, but they were sufficient to season the whole earth, as a little salt or a tiny bit of leaven is enough. They and their message would persevere and endure, as salt is the great conserver, the image of permanence. Jesus went on immediately, in Matthew's Gospel, to use an image of light. The two metaphors are connected both by opposition (salt is in the earth, light must be raised on high; salt is tasted while light is seen) and by similarity, for salt has always been associated with fire and brightness.

Salt, once isolated, is white and glittering. It is the opposite of wet. You win it by freeing it from water with the help of fire and the sun, and it dries out flesh. Eating salt causes thirst. Dryness, in the pre-Socratic cosmic system which still informs our imagery, is always connected with fire, heat, and light.

For the alchemists, common salt (one of the elements of matter) was neither masculine nor feminine but neuter: the edible rock always has something a little inhuman about it; it disconcertingly sits astride categories. Salt does have to do with sex, however, because it is a dynamic substance which both alters itself and causes change. Like sex, it is exciting and dangerous and gives pleasure. Salt comes out of the sea like the goddess of sex, Aphrodite, whose name the ancient Greeks thought meant "sea-foam-born." In European folk custom, impotence has traditionally been cured by a hilarious, bawdy salting of the disobliging member by a crowd of women.

Often priests or mourners or people who are in a state of crisis—those whom society has marginalized, for whatever reason—must observe a taboo on salt. Eating no salt, which is often accompanied by sexual continence, means a fight to maintain equilibrium at a time of turbulence and difficulty, when one has no need of the dynamic. It also means that one has left society, rejecting the enticements and the comforts of civilization, or that one intends to dramatize a profound discontent with the way society is conducting itself.

Salt represents the civilized: it requires know-how to get it, and a sophisticated combination of cooking and spoilt, jaded appetites to need it. Its sharp taste suggests sharpness of intellect and liveliness of mind. Salt (bright, dry, titillating, and dynamic) is synonymous in several languages with wit and wisdom.

It preserves things from corruption—even as it corrodes other things with its bite. A little of it fertilizes the land; a lot sterilizes it. Because salt stops rot and because it is fiery, salt is intrinsically pure. It is the child of the sun and the sea, two basic symbols of cleanliness and purity. Salt keeps meat safe for the winter and so feeds man; it is, therefore, a blessing. Salt also means barrenness, and it is, therefore, used for cursing. Its imperishable rock-nature, and its purity and wisdom, make it the material of oaths and covenants, which guarantee, if the swearer breaks his oath, that malediction will fall upon him.

Salt as covenant-sealer signifies friendship and hospitality. The silver saltcellar was a central and often highly decorative ornament on the banquet tables of all rich European families: it marked off the close friends of the family from those "below the salt," who were not considered worthy of such intimacy. When someone inadvertently spills salt, it is considered unlucky because it signifies enmity and malediction. Leonardo da Vinci followed this tradition in his fresco of *The Last Supper* when he depicted Judas as upsetting the saltcellar.

Here as before, however, salt is powerfully contradictory: because it is pure and strong, it counteracts malediction. Witches hate salt. They never served it at their Sabbaths, and if you put some under a witch's cushion she could not sit down: this was considered a surefire method of finding out whether someone was a witch or not. Devils also detest it. Therefore, if you are unlucky enough to spill salt, all you have to do is throw some over your left shoulder (where all bad spirits congregate) and the evil will be undone. An owl's cry is a malediction: to neutralize it, one has to sprinkle salt on the bird's tail.

Until recently, salt was part of the Roman Catholic baptismal ceremony (Luther banned it as Popish superstition). A few grains were placed on the baby's tongue to signify purity, endurance, wisdom, power, uniqueness ("You are the salt of the earth"), and protection from evil. It was a sign of God's friendship and his power over Satan.

CARÊME DINNER

By Lady Morgan

Lady Morgan, born Sydney Owenson in Dublin; was a novelist as well as a travel writer. O'Donnel published in 1814, was admired by Maria Edgeworth, Mary Russell Mitford and Sir Walter Scott. She wrote two books on life in France in 1817 and 1829, and published another on Italy in 1821.

We happened to have with us two noted Amphitryons, (English and French) when a dinner invitation from Monsieur et Madame de Rothschild was brought in by the servant. '*Quel bonheur,*' exclaimed my French friend, as I read aloud. 'You are going to dine at the first table in France;—in Europe. You are going to judge, from your own personal experience, of the genius of Carême.'

'In England,' said my British Apicius, 'I remember immense prices being given for his second-hand *pâtés*, after they had made their appearance at the Regent's table.'

Anecdotes beyond number were then given of the pomps and vanities of the life of Carême; the number of the aids attached to his staff; his box at the opera, and other proofs of sumptuosity and taste, which, whether true or false, were very amusing; and increased my desire to make the acquaintance, through his 'oeuvres complettes,' of a man who was at the head of his class …

To do justice to the science and research of a dinner so served, would require a knowledge of the art equal to that which produced it. Its character, however, was, that it was in season, that it was up to its time, that it was in the spirit of the age, that there was no *perruque* in its composition, no trace of the wisdom of our ancestors in a single dish; no high-spiced sauces, no dark-brown gravies, no flavour of cayenne and allspice, no tincture of catsup and walnut pickle, no visible agency of those vulgar elements of cooking, of the good old times, fire and water. Distillations of the most delicate viands, extracted in 'silver dews,' with chemical precision.

'On tepid clouds of rising steam,' formed the *fond* of all. Every meat presented its own natural aroma; every vegetable its own shade of verdure. The *mayonese* was fried in ice, (like Ninon's description of Sévigné's heart,) and the tempered chill of the *plombière* (which held the place of the eternal *fondu* and *soufflets* of our English tables) anticipated the stronger shock, and broke it, of the exquisite *avalanche*, which, with the hue and odour of fresh gathered nectarines, satisfied every sense, and dissipated every coarser flavour.

With less genius than went to the composition of this dinner, men have written epic poems; and if crowns were distributed to cooks, as to actors, the wreath of Pasta or Sontag, (divine as *they* are,) were never more fairly won than the laurel which should have graced the brow of Carême, for this specimen of the intellectual perfection of an art, the standard and gauge of modern civilization! On good cookery, depends good health; on good health, depends the permanence of a good organization; and on these, the whole excellence in the structure of human society. Cruelty, violence, and barbarism, were the characteristics of the men who fed upon the tough fibres of half-dressed oxen. Humanity, knowledge, and refinement belong to the living generation, whose tastes and temperance are regulated by the science of such philosophers as Carême, and such amphitryons as his employers.

As I was seated next to Monsieur Rothschild, I took occasion to insinuate, after the soup, (for who would utter a word before?) that I was not wholly unworthy of a place at a table served by Carême; that I was already acquainted with the merits of the man who had first declared against '*la cuisine epicée et aromatisée;*' and that though I had been accused of a tendency towards *the bonnet rouge*, my true vocation was the *bonnet blanc*. I had, I said, long *gouté les ouvrages de Monsieur Carême* theoretically; and that now a practical acquaintance with them, filled me with a still higher admiration for his unrivalled talents.

'*Eh! bien,*' said Monsieur Rothschild, laughing, 'he, on his side, has also relished your works; and here is a proof of it.'

I really blush, like Sterne's accusing spirit, as I give in the fact: but he pointed to a column of the most ingenious confectionary architecture, on which my name was inscribed in spun sugar. *My* name written in sugar! Ye Quarterlies and Blackwoods, and *tu Brute*, false and faithless Westminster!—ye who have never traced my proscribed name but in gall,—think of 'Lady Morgan' in sugar; and that, too, at a table surrounded by some of the great supporters of the holy alliance!—*je n'en revenais pas!*

All I could do, under my triumphant emotion, I did. I begged to be introduced to the celebrated and flattering artist, and promised, should I ever again trouble the public with my idleness, to devote a tributary page to his genius, and to my sense of his merits, literary and culinary. Carême was sent for after coffee, and was presented to me, in the vestibule of the chateau, by his master. He was a well-bred gentlemen, perfectly free from pedantry, and, when we had mutually complimented each other on our respective works, he bowed himself out, and got into his carriage, which was waiting to take him to Paris.

Lady Morgan in France, ED. Elizabeth Sudderby
and P. J. Yarrow, 1971

THE LEADING WARM SAUCES

By Auguste Escoffier

WARM sauces are of two kinds: the leading sauces, also called "mother sauces," and the small sauces, which are usually derived from the first-named, and are generally only modified forms thereof. Cooking stock only includes the leading sauces, but I shall refer to the small hot sauces and the cold sauces at the end of the auxiliary stock.

Experience, which plays such an important part in culinary work, is nowhere so necessary as in the preparation of sauces, for not only must the latter flatter the palate, but they must also vary in savour, consistence and viscosity, in accordance with the dishes they accompany. By this means, in a well-ordered dinner, each dish differs from the preceding ones and from those that follow.

Furthermore, sauces must, through the perfection of their preparation, obey the general laws of a rational hygiene, wherefore they should be served and combined in such wise as to allow of easy digestion by the frequently disordered stomachs of their consumers.

Carême was quite justified in pluming himself upon the fact that during his stay at the English Court his master—the Prince Regent—had assured him that he (Carême) was the only one among those who had served his Highness whose cooking had been at all easy of digestion. Carême had grasped the essential truth that the richer the cooking is, the more speedily do the stomach and palate tire of it. And, indeed, it is a great mistake to suppose that, in order to do good cooking, it is necessary to be prodigal in one's use of all things. In reality, practice dictates fixed and regular quantities, and from these one cannot diverge without upsetting the hygienic and sapid equilibrium on which the value of a sauce depends. The requisite quantities of each ingredient must, of course, be used, but neither more nor less, as there are objections to either extreme.

Any sauce whatsoever should be smooth, light (without being liquid), glossy to the eye, and decided in taste. When these conditions are fulfilled it is always easy to digest even for tired stomachs.

An essential point in the making of sauces is the seasoning, and it would be impossible for me to lay sufficient stress on the importance of not indulging in any excess in this respect. It too often happens that the insipidity of a badly-made sauce is corrected by excessive seasoning; this is an absolutely deplorable practice.

Seasoning should be so calculated as to be merely a complementary factor, which, though it must throw the savour of dishes into relief, may not form a recognisable part of them. If it be excessive, it modifies and even destroys the taste peculiar to every dish—to the great detriment of the latter and of the consumer's health.

It is therefore desirable that each sauce should possess its own special flavour, well defined, the result of the combined flavours of all its ingredients.

If, in the making of sauces, one allowed oneself to be guided by those principles which are the very foundation of good cookery, the general denunciation of sauces by the medical faculty would be averted; and this denunciation no sauce deserves if it be carefully prepared, conformably with the laws prescribed by practice and its resulting experience.

THE ROUX

The roux being the cohering element of leading sauces, it is necessary to reveal its preparation and constituents before giving one's attention to the latter.

Three kinds of roux are used—namely, brown roux, for brown sauces; pale roux, for veloutés, or cream sauces; and white roux, for white sauces and Béchamel.

19—Brown Roux

Quantities for making about One lb.—Eight oz. of clarified butter, nine oz. of best-quality flour.

Preparation.—Mix the flour and butter in a very thick stew-pan, and put it on the side of the fire or in a moderate oven. Stir the mixture repeatedly so that the heat may be evenly distributed throughout the whole of its volume.

The time allowed for the cooking of brown roux cannot be precisely determined, as it depends upon the degree of heat employed. The more intense the latter, the speedier will be the cooking, while the stirring will of necessity be more rapid. Brown roux is known to be cooked when it has acquired a fine, light brown colour, and when it exudes a scent resembling that of the hazel-nut, characteristic of baked flour.

It is very, important that brown roux should not be cooked too rapidly. As a matter of fact, among the various constituent elements of flour, the starch alone acts as the cohering principle. This starch is contained in little cells, which tightly constrain it, but which are sufficiently porous to permit the percolation of liquid and fatty substances. Under the influence of moderate heat and the infiltered butter, the cells burst through the swelling of the starch, and the latter thereupon completely combines with the butter to form a mass capable of absorbing six times its own weight of liquid when cooked.

When the cooking takes place with a very high initial heat the starch gets burned within its shrivelled cells, and swelling is then possible only in those parts which have been least burned.

The cohering principle is thus destroyed, and double or treble the quantity of roux becomes necessary in order to obtain the required consistency. But this excess of roux in the sauce chokes it up without binding it, and prevents it from despumating or becoming clear. At the same time, the cellulose and the burnt starch lend a bitterness to the sauce of which no subsequent treatment can rid it.

From the above it follows that, starch being the only one from among the different constituents of flour which really effects the coherence of sauces, there would be considerable advantage in preparing roux either from a pure form of it, or from substances with kindred properties, such as fecula, arrowroot, etc. It is only habit that causes flour to be still used as the cohering element of roux, and, indeed, the hour is not so far distant when the advantages of the changes I propose will be better understood—changes which have been already recommended by Favre in his dictionary.

With a roux well made from the purest starch—in which case the volume of starch and butter would equal about half that of the flour and butter of the old method—and with strong and succulent brown stock, a Spanish sauce or Espagnole may be made in one hour. And this sauce will be clearer, more brilliant, and better than that of the old processes, which needed three days at least to despumate.

20—Pale Roux

The quantities are the same as for brown roux, but cooking must cease as soon as the colour of the roux begins to change, and before the appearance of any colouring whatsoever.

The observations I made relative to brown roux, concerning the cohering element, apply also to pale roux.

21—White Roux

Same quantities as for brown and pale roux, but the time of cooking is limited to a few minutes, as it is only needful, in this case, to do away with the disagreeable taste of raw flour which is typical of those sauces whose roux has not been sufficiently cooked.

22—Brown Sauce or Espagnole

Quantities Required for Four Quarts.—One lb. of brown roux dissolved in a tall, thick saucepan with six quarts of brown stock or estouffade. Put the saucepan on an open fire, and stir the sauce with a spatula or a whisk, and do not leave it until it begins to boil. Then remove the spatula, and put the saucepan on a corner of the fire, letting it lean slightly to one side with the help of a wedge, so that boiling may only take place at one point, and that the inert principles thrown out by the sauce during despumation may accumulate high up in the saucepan, whence they can be easily removed as they collect.

It is advisable during despumation to change saucepans twice or even three times, straining every time, and adding a quart of brown stock to replace what has evaporated. At length, when the sauce begins to get lighter, and about two hours before finally straining it, two lbs. of fresh tomatoes, roughly cut up, should be added, or an equivalent quantity of tomato purée, and about one lb. of *Mirepoix*, prepared according to Formula No. 228. The sauce is then reduced so as to measure four quarts when strained, after which it is poured into a wide tureen, and must be kept in motion until quite cool lest a skin should form on its surface.

The time required for the despumation of an Espagnole varies according to the quality of the stock and roux. We saw above that one hour sufficed for a concentrated stock and starch roux, in which case the Mirepoix and the tomato are inserted from the first. But much more time is required if one is dealing with a roux whose base is flour. In the latter case six hours should be allowed, provided one have excellent stock and well-made roux. More often than not this work is done in two stages, thus: after having despumated the Espagnole for six or eight hours the first day, it is put on the fire the next day with half its volume of stock, and it is left to despumate a few hours more before it is finally strained.

Summing up my opinion on this subject, I can only give my colleagues the following advice, based upon long experience :

1. Only use strong, clear stock with a decided taste.
2. Be scrupulously careful of the roux, however it may be made. By following these two rules, a clear, brilliant, and consistent Espagnole will always be obtained in a fairly short time.

23—Half Glaze

This is the Espagnole sauce, having reached the limit of perfection by final despumation. It is obtained by reducing one quart of Espagnole and one quart of first-class brown stock until its volume is reduced to nine-tenths of a quart. It is then strained into a *bain-marie* of convenient dimensions, and it is finished, away from the fire, with one-tenth of a quart of excellent sherry. Cover the *bain-marie*, or slightly butter the top to avoid the formation of a skin. This sauce is the base of all the smaller brown sauces.

24—Lenten Espagnole

Practical men are not agreed as to the need of Lenten Espagnole. The ordinary Espagnole being really a neutral sauce in flavour, it is quite simple to give it the necessary flavour by the addition of the required quantity of fish *fumet*. It is only, therefore, when one wishes to conform with the demands of a genuine Lent sauce that a fish Espagnole is needed. And, certainly in this case, nothing can take its place.

The preparation of this Espagnole does not differ from that of the ordinary kind, except that the bacon is replaced by mushroom parings in the Mirepoix, and that the sauce must be despumated for only one hour.

This sauce takes the place of the ordinary Espagnole, for Lenten preparations, in every case where the latter is generally used, in Gratins, in the Genevoise sauce, etc.

25—Ordinary Velouté Sauce

Quantities Required for Four Quarts.—One lb. of pale roux (Formula 20), five quarts of white veal stock (Formula 10).

Dissolve the roux in the cold white veal stock and put the saucepan containing this mixture on an open fire, stirring the sauce with a spatula or whisk, so as to avoid its burning at the bottom. Add one oz. of table-salt, a pinch of nutmeg and white powdered pepper, together with one-quarter lb. of nice white mushroom parings, if these are handy. Now boil and move to a corner of the fire to despumate slowly for one and a half hours, at the same time observing the precautions advised for ordinary Espagnole (Formula 22). Strain through muslin into a smaller saucepan, add one pint of white stock, and despumate for another half hour. Strain it again through a tammy or a sieve into a wide tureen, and keep moving it with a spatula until it is quite cold.

I am not partial to garnishing Velouté Sauce with carrots, an onion with a clove stuck into it, and a faggot, as many do. The stock should be sufficiently fragrant of itself, without requiring the addition of anything beyond the usual condiments. The only exception I should make would be for mushroom parings, even though it is preferable, when possible, to replace these by mushroom liquor. But this is always scarce in kitchens where it is used for other purposes; wherefore it is often imperative to have recourse to parings in its stead. The latter may not, however, be added to the stock itself, as they would blacken it; hence I advise their addition to the Velouté during its preparation.

26—Velouté De Volaille

This is identical with ordinary Velouté except that instead of having white veal stock for its liquor, it is diluted with white poultry stock. The mode of procedure and the time allowed for cooking are the same.

26a—Fish Velouté

Velouté is the base of various fish sauces whose recipes will be given in Part II.

Prepare it in precisely the same way as poultry velouté but instead of using poultry stock, use very clear fish *fumet*, and let it despumate for twenty minutes only. (See fish *fumet* No. 11.)

27—Allemande Sauce Or Thickened Velouté

Allemande Sauce is not, strictly speaking, a basic sauce. However, it is so often resorted to in the preparation of other sauces that I think it necessary to give it after the Veloutés, from which it is derived.

Quantities Required for One Quart.

The yolks of 5 eggs.	½ the juice of a lemon.
1 pint of cold white stock.	¼ pint of mushroom liquor.
1 quart of Velouté, well despumated.	

Mode of Procedure.—Put the various ingredients in a thick-bottomed sauté-pan and mix them carefully. Then put the pan on an open fire, and stir the sauce with a metal spatula, lest it burn at the bottom. When the sauce has been reduced to about one quart, add one-third pint of fresh cream to it, and reduce further for a few minutes. It should then be passed through a fine strainer into a tureen and kept moving until quite cold.

Prepared thus, the Allemande Sauce is ready for the preparation of the smaller sauces. Butter must only be added at the very last moment, for if it were buttered any earlier it would most surely turn. The same injunction holds good with this sauce when it is to be served in its original state; it should then receive a small addition of cream, and be buttered so that it may attain its required delicacy; but this addition of butter and cream ought only to be made at the last moment, and away from the fire. When a sauce thickened with egg yolks has any fat substance added to it, it cannot be exposed to a higher temperature than 140 degrees Fahrenheit without risking decomposition.

28—Bechamel Sauce

Quantities Required for Four Quarts.

1 lb. of white roux.	⅔ oz. of salt, 1 pinch of mignonette, and grated nutmeg, and 1 small spring of thyme
4 ½ quarts of boiling; milk.	
½ lb. of lean veal.	1 minced onion.

Preparation.—Pour the boiling milk on the roux, which should be almost cold, and whisk it well so as to avoid lumps. Let it boil, then cook on the side of the fire. Meanwhile the lean veal should have been cut into small cubes, and fried with butter in a saucepan, together with the minced onion. When the veal has stiffened without becoming coloured, it is added to the Béchamel, together with salt and the other aromatics. Let the sauce boil slowly for about one hour in all, and then pass it through a tammy into a tureen; butter the top, lest a crust should form.

When Béchamel is intended for Lenten preparations, the veal must be omitted.

There is another way of making the sauce. After having boiled the milk, the seasoning and aromatics should be added; the saucepan is then covered and placed on a corner of the stove, so as to ensure a thorough infusion. The boiling milk must now be poured on to the roux which has been separately prepared, and the sauce should then cook for one quarter of an hour only.

29—Tomato Sauce

Quantities Required for Four Quarts.

5 oz. of salted breast of pork, rather fat.

6 oz. of carrots cut into cubes.

6 oz. of onions cut into cubes.
1 bay leaf and 1 small sprig of thyme.
5 oz. of flour.

2 oz. of butter, ½ oz. of salt, 1 oz. of sugar, a pinch of pepper.
10 lbs. of raw tomatoes or 4 quarts of same, mashed.

2 quarts of white stock.

Preparation.—Fry the pork with the butter in a tall, thick-bottomed saucepan. When the pork is nearly melted, add the carrots, onions, and aromatics. Cook and stir the vegetables, then add the flour, which should be allowed to cook until it begins to brown. Now put in the tomatoes and white stock, mix the whole well, and set to boil on an open fire. At this point add the seasoning and a crushed clove of garlic, cover the saucepan, and place in a moderate oven, where it may cook for one and one-half hours. At the end of this time the sauce should be passed through a sieve or tammy, and it should boil while being stirred. Finally, pour it into a tureen, and butter its surface to avoid the formation of a skin.

Remarks.—A purée of tomatoes is also used in cookery; it is prepared in precisely the same fashion, except that the flour is omitted and only one pint of white stock is added.

30—Hollandaise Sauce

Quantities Required for One Quart.—One and one-half lbs. of butter, the yolks of six eggs, one pinch of mignonette pepper and one-quarter oz. of salt, three tablespoonfuls of good vinegar.

Preparation.—Put the salt, the mignonette, the vinegar, and as much water in a small saucepan, and reduce by three-quarters on the fire. Move the saucepan to a corner of the fire or into a *bain-marie*, and add a spoonful of fresh water and the yolks. Work the whole with a whisk until the yolks thicken and have the consistence of cream. Then remove the saucepan to a tepid place and gradually pour the butter on the yolks while briskly stirring the sauce. When the butter is absorbed, the sauce ought to be thick and firm. It is brought to the correct consistence with a little water, which also lightens it slightly, but the addition of water is optional. The sauce is completed by a drop of lemon juice, and it is rubbed through a tammy.

Remarks.—The consistence of sauces whose processes are identical with those of the Hollandaise may be varied at will; for instance, the number of yolks may be increased if a very thick sauce is desired, and it may be lessened in the reverse case. Also similar results may be obtained by cooking the eggs either more or less. As a rule, if a thick sauce be required, the yolks ought to be well cooked and the sauce kept almost cold in the making. Experience alone—the fruit of long practice—can teach the various devices which enable the skilled worker to obtain different results from the same kind and quality of material.

Fernand Point's Notebook

By Thomas Keller and Fernand Point

INTRODUCTION

I recall the day very clearly. I was working at the Dunes Club in Narragansett, Rhode Island, when my mentor Roland Henin lent me his copy of *Ma Gastronomie*. He said it was a special book—his favorite. He was right. It was just extraordinary. I took it everywhere with me for two years and read it whenever I had a moment to spare. I considered it overextended borrowing but Chef Henin never asked for it back. I finally returned his copy when I received one as a present in 1979.

Ma Gastronomie elevated my determination to cook. Before then, the greatest pleasure I received from working in the kitchen came from the act of repetition. I found satisfaction from the challenge of perfecting all my tasks. I would make a Hollandaise or filet a piece of salmon, for instance, and look forward to doing them over again the next day with the goal of becoming better—even just a little—each time. Through Chef Point's words I finally understood and discovered a higher sense of purpose for my chosen profession: cooking was not just about technique and providing sustenance; it was about nurturing.

Ma Gastronomie was also pivotal in my decision to work in France. It awakened my desire to learn how to be a better cook and to train under its Michelin starred chefs. It was a defining moment; realizing who I was and what I would aspire to become. Cooking was not about a career, it was a lifestyle. I decided to model my life after these chefs.

I have always suggested that readers enjoy *Ma Gastronomie* as they would consume a great meal. It is imperative to relish slowly every moment and every word of Chef Point's philosophies, along with his genuine and humorous narratives. However, what has always stood out in my mind was the manner by which he wrote his recipes. They were almost a story within themselves. Often written without specific directions or ingredient amounts, they intrigued and always made me want to cook even more. His recipes made me understand that the techniques I used while making those dishes were directly proportional to the level of cooking I was doing at that moment. Every time I improved, my interpretation and execution of that dish also evolved and became better. In my mind, this meant that these dishes were no longer Chef Point's recipes. The title "Ma Gastronomie"—my gastronomy—became a recollection of my personal journeys and skills as a cook. I had transformed these recipes and made them my own.

When Tracy Carns, the publisher of The Rookery Press, initially reached out to gauge my interest in helping write the foreword for the reprinting of *Ma Gastronomie*, I said yes without hesitation. I found the notion both humbling and exciting. This was a book that that had such an impact on my life and my career, and was a resource I fell back on without fail. A true gourmand, Chef Point imparted knowledge and inspiration generously to legions of aspiring cooks. He played a vital role in the resurgence of French cuisine; its renaissance established "nouvelle cuisine" in the 80s and catapulted many chefs into the public consciousness. Under his tutelage, many of his apprentices including Chefs Paul Bocuse, Pierre and Jean Troisgros and Alain Chapel, were able to step out and establish successful kitchens of their own. And while *Ma Gastronomie* was first published almost forty years ago, I believe his philosophies are still very much relevant today and his legacy of mentorship stronger than ever.

Being a mentor is about creating an impact on young cooks. They translate the knowledge you impart into something that is meaningful to you, and yet still meaningful to them. It is a philosophy I hold dearly and one that plays a significant role at our restaurants: we challenge and teach our cooks constantly so that they never stop growing and have many opportunities before them.

Putting *Ma Gastronomie* back into circulation is incredible news. It is very likely that the crop of young talent we have today will realize Chef's Point's genius and transform this new-found knowledge to their own brand of creativity in their kitchens. I cannot wait to see what happens next.

Recently, I asked Chef Henin what motivated him to share his favorite book with me on that fateful day. His words are unforgettable ... He said that there were times he would observe me working in the kitchen, and he would notice how happy and contented I appeared. It did not matter whether I was having a good day or a bad day ... I looked like I belonged. He said it was during those moments that he was reminded of an old French proverb:

A toi, cuisine devant l'enfer de tes fourneaux parfois je découvre le paradis sur terre.

"To you, kitchen, facing your oven's inferno, I sometimes discover paradise on earth."

—Thomas Keller
The French Laundry
August 2008

Fernand Point kept a small cream-colored notebook in which he jotted down his thoughts on cuisine and life—in his case, the two were synonymous. These notes constitute a kind of gastronomic testament as well as a line of conduct to be followed by young cuisiniers:

It is with my stoves that I people my silences.

"Silence is golden," they say—and yet, cuisine, one must speak of that!

The cuisinier loses his reputation when he becomes indifferent to his work.

Man is not a machine, and a cuisinier sometimes gets tired. But the clients must never know it.

The timetable for the meals of the restaurant staff should be as strict as that of the railroads.

Cuisine is not invariable like a Codex formula, but one must be careful not to modify the essential bases.

As far as cuisine is concerned one must read everything, see everything, hear everything, try everything, observe everything, in order to retain, in the end, just a little bit!

One is not born a *rôtisseur* (roasting chef), as Brillat-Savarin said, but one becomes one just as one becomes a cuisinier.

Willingness and good intentions cannot replace competence in the management of a restaurant.

Butter! Give me butter! Always butter!

Even if certain guests make "frown soup," always keep a smile.

La grande cuisine must not wait for the guest; it's the guest who must wait for *la grande cuisine.*

A good meal should be as harmonious as a symphony and as well built as a Romanesque cathedral.

The most difficult dishes to make generally appear to be the simplest.

That which is very simple is not necessarily the least delectable. Take, for instance, sauerkraut. Yet, you still have to know how to prepare it.

Inattention never pays off in the kitchen.

What is a *béarnaise* sauce? An egg yolk, some shallots, some tarragon. But believe me, it requires years of practice for the result to be perfect! Take your eyes off it for an instant and it will be unusable.

After one cocktail or, worse yet, two, the palate can no more distinguish a bottle of Château Mouton-Rothschild from a bottle of ink!

All men fraternize at the table, especially when one has enchanted their souls.

FONDUE DU FLEUVE-ROI

(Fondue "King River")

This recipe is named in honor of the Rhône, the "King River," which is magnificent at Vienne.

Rub a fireproof glazed earthenware casserole with a clove of garlic. Add 4 cups (1 litre) of dry white wine from Château Grillet, and a 1 1/2-pound (675 g) mixture of rich Gruyère cheese and Emmenthal cheese. Cut the cheese into the casserole and add a piece of butter. Place the casserole on an alcohol burner and stir constantly until the cheese melts completely and has the consistency of smooth, thick cream.

Blend a little flour and a pinch of pepper into 1/2 cup (125 ml) of kirsch and add to the fondue. Serve with cubes of bread to dip into the fondue. This recipe will serve four persons.

POTAGE AUX FÈVES FRAÎCHES

(Fresh Fava Soup)

Cook 1 pound (500 g) of freshly hulled green fava or broad beans, 4 ounces (125 g) of chopped lean bacon, and one sprig of savory in 2 quarts (2 litres) of water for about one hour. Strain through a fine sieve, add some butter and serve with toasted croutons. This recipe will serve four.

SOUPE DE POISSONS DES MARINIERS

(Fishermen's Fish Soup)

Marinate 6 pounds (2.75 kg) of cleaned fish from the Rhône (freshwater fish) for twelve hours in a marinade of white wine, fennel, salt, pepper, and 1/4 cup (60 ml) of anise liqueur. Poach the fish in the marinade, adding white wine until it almost covers the fish. Remove the fish, add 3 ladlesful of fresh chopped tomato, and let this simmer for about one-half hour. Strain through a fine sieve and reduce the cooking liquid. Return the boned fish to the soup, add 3 ladlesful of cream, enrich it with butter and, at the last moment, add the juice of a lemon. Correct the seasoning and serve. This recipe will serve six persons.

VELOUTÉ DE GAUDES

(Corn Meal Velouté)

In the Bressan dialect, "gaudes" refers to corn flour or corn meal. The natives of the region of Ain eat a great deal of corn meal, one of the reasons they're often called "ventres jaunes"—yellow bellies.

Slice 3 onions very finely and cook them in butter until they are slightly golden. Mix a small amount of chicken broth into a ladleful of corn meal to make a paste and add to the onions with more chicken broth. Beat vigorously and simmer for one-half hour. Add 2 cups (500 ml) of *crème fraîche*, correct the seasoning and serve very hot. This recipe will make four servings.

TRUITE AU BEURRE MOUSSEUX

(Trout In Foamed Butter)

Place some fresh thyme and parsley inside a cleaned 4-pound (1.75 kg) trout. Season lightly and let it rest for twenty-four hours. Remove the thyme and parsley. Prepare a moderately firm eel stuffing with herbs and stuff the trout.

Cook the trout *meunière*. Use enough butter to half cover the fish and baste it frequently. At the last moment, place the trout in the oven to firm the stuffing. Serve it very hot in some foamed butter with lemon juice added.

TRUITE AUX CHAMPIGNONS

(Trout With Mushrooms)

Clean a brook trout weighing about 2 pounds (1 kg) and cook it *meunière*. In a flameproof pan sauté in butter a thick layer of sliced mushrooms flavored with *fines herbes*. Arrange the cooked trout on the sautéed mushrooms and pour the butter from the trout over both. Cover the trout and mushrooms completely with a *duxelles* seasoned with shallots (or with finely chopped *fines herbes*). Sprinkle with bread crumbs, dot with butter and brown in the oven for a few minutes.

Serve the trout very hot along with a separate sauceboat containing *beurre noisette* seasoned with shallots.

TRUITE EN PÂTE

(Trout In Pastry)

Clean and skin a trout. Wrap the fish in a layer of flaky puff pastry made with fresh butter and bake in a moderate oven for fifteen minutes. Serve with a *béarnaise* sauce made without shallots and garnish the dish with crayfish tails cooked in crayfish butter.

TRUITE POCHÉE FERNAND GRAVEY

(Poached Trout Fernand Gravey)

Season the inside of a cleaned trout with salt and some herbs. Roll the fish in buttered paper and poach in a dry white wine with some mushroom broth added.

Transfer the cooked trout to a warm platter and reduce the cooking liquid by one quarter, adding some heavy cream. For two parts of this sauce add one part *hollandaise* sauce, along with a little crayfish butter and some mushroom-truffle purée cooked very slightly in a little butter. Correct the seasoning, if necessary.

Remove the paper from the trout, coat the fish with the sauce, and decorate it with fluted mushrooms, cooked crayfish tails and some whole, curled crayfish. Serve piping hot with the sauce in a separate sauceboat.

TURBOT AU CHAMPAGNE

(Turbot In Champagne)

Place slices of turbot in a buttered skillet and top them with some peeled, seeded, and coarsely chopped tomatoes and some chopped parsley. Add just enough Champagne to cover the fish and cook for about ten minutes. Remove the fish to a warm platter and reduce the sauce until it has thickened itself. Add a large spoonful of *crime fraîche* to the sauce and season. Spoon the sauce over the turbot and serve.

AUBERGINES DÉBOTTÉES
(Molded Eggplant)

Peel 8 small eggplant and cut them into thick slices. Salt the slices and let them rest for one hour to remove most of their moisture. Pat the slices dry and cook them in butter or olive oil in a covered casserole till just tender. Drain and put them through a sieve or food mill. Add 1/2 cup (125 ml) of milk and 3 lightly beaten eggs. Do not add pepper.

Arrange the mixture in a buttered mold and cook ten or fifteen minutes in a *bain-marie* in a moderate oven. Unmold, spoon a tomato sauce over the top and serve.

AUBERGINES AUX TOMATES
(Eggplant With Tomatoes)

Prepare a very thick, well-seasoned tomato sauce. While the sauce is cooking, peel the eggplant and dry the slices well. Cook these in a pan with butter, a little salt and some pepper.

In a shallow ovenproof dish arrange a layer of eggplant, a layer of tomato sauce, and a layer of thick, heavy cream. Place in the oven to brown and serve very hot.

CARDONS HENRI CLOS-JOUVE
(Cardoons Henri Clos-fouve)

Use the white part or hearts of cardoons (large edible thistles related to the artichoke). Wipe well, but do not wash, and cut into small sticks. Cook the cardoons in a blanc consisting of 1 quart (1 litre) of water, 1 tbsp of flour dissolved in some cold vinegar, the juice of half a lemon and a good pinch of salt. Prepare a light *roux*, adding 2 ladlesful of the blanc, 2 ladlesful of *crème fraîche*, and season with 1 salted anchovy, mashed and thoroughly blended into some hot butter.

Mix the cardoon slices with some sliced truffles. Spoon the sauce over the mixture, place in a hot oven for a few minutes and serve piping hot.

SOUFFLÉ DE CAROTTES

(Carrot Soufflé)

Thoroughly drain 2 pounds (1 kg) of carrots which have been cooked in salted water and put them through a strainer or food mill. Sauté the strained carrots in a pan with some butter over high heat to remove all moisture. Off heat, add 3 egg yolks, salt, pepper, butter, parsley and a little *béchamel* sauce to the carrots. Gently fold in 3 beaten egg whites.

Turn the carrot mixture into a buttered mold, place in a *bain-marie* and cook in a moderate oven for thirty minutes. Unmold and sprinkle lightly with some good meat juices before serving.

CHAMPIGNONS FARCIS

(Stuffed Mushrooms)

"Bread crumbs always enhance the taste of fresh mushrooms."

Remove the stems from about 30 large mushrooms. Wash but do not peel them. To prepare the stuffing, soak approximately 5 thin slices of bread in milk. Gently squeeze the moisture from the bread and crumble the slices into a pan with 6 tbsp (90 g) of melted butter. Sauté the bread crumbs and butter, adding one beaten egg, some *fines herbes*, salt, pepper, and some mashed cooked foie gras.

Fill the mushrooms with the stuffing and place them in a well-buttered shallow oven-proof dish. Dot with butter and bake in a moderate oven for ten minutes.

SAUCES

By Michel Guérard

COLD SAUCES

Sauce vinaigrette minceur I

FRENCH DRESSING

To serve four:

1 tablespoon of olive oil
5 tablespoons of **chicken stock (5)**
1 tablespoon of red-wine vinegar
1 tablespoon of lemon juice
Salt and pepper

NOTE: For *vinaigrettes*, you should use real homemade stock, which has the gelatin content lacking in canned or bouillon-cube broths.

Combine the ingredients in a small bowl and mix well with a fork.

Sauce vinaigrette minceur II

FRENCH DRESSING WITH HERBS

To serve four:

- 1 tablespoon of olive oil
- 5 tablespoons of **chicken stock (5)**
- 1 whole clove of garlic, peeled
- ½ teaspoon of minced fresh tarragon
- ½ teaspoon of minced fresh chervil or parsley
- 2 leaves of fresh basil, minced
- 1 tablespoon of sherry vinegar
- 1 tablespoon of lemon juice
- Salt and pepper

Combine the olive oil, stock, garlic, and herbs in a small bowl, and let them marinate together for 2 hours. Add the vinegar, lemon juice, and salt and pepper, and mix well with a fork.

Sauce préférée

THE PREFERRED MINCEUR SALAD DRESSING

To serve four:

- 5 tablespoons of **fromage blanc (173)**
- 2 tablespoons of wine vinegar
- 1 tablespoon of soy sauce
- 1 teaspoon of Dijon mustard
- 1 teaspoon of minced fresh herbs (chervil, tarragon, parsley, chives)
- Salt sparingly to taste
- Pepper

Mix all the ingredients together in a bowl with a whisk, or in an electric blender.

Sauce mayonnaise minceur I

LOW-CALORIE MAYONNAISE

This recipe makes a very light mayonnaise, which, however, should be used sparingly, as it does contain both egg yolk and oil. To make about 1 ¼ cups:

> 1 egg, separated
> 1 ½ teaspoons of light-colored mustard (Dijon)
> ¼ teaspoon of salt
> A grinding of white pepper, or a pinch of cayenne
> 2 tablespoons of peanut oil
> 2 tablespoons of olive oil
> 1 teaspoon of lemon juice
> 2 level tablespoons of **fromage blanc (173)**
> The egg white, beaten

In a bowl and with a whisk, or with an electric beater, beat together the egg yolk, mustard, salt, and pepper. Then very slowly add the 4 tablespoons of oil, beating constantly. As the mixture thickens, add the lemon juice a few drops at a time to thin out the sauce a little. When all the oil has been added, gently stir in the *fromage blanc.*

NOTE: *The recipe may be prepared ahead to this point. Shortly before serving, beat the egg white, and fold it gently into the mayonnaise. Since you may not need the full quantity of the recipe at one time, you may fold only half the beaten white into half the quantity of mayonnaise, and save the remaining sauce to use another time with a freshly beaten white. See* **sauce mayonnaise (13)** *concerning refrigeration. Ed.*

Sauce mayonnaise minceur II
LOW-CALORIE MAYONNAISE WITH PURÉED VEGETABLES

The recipe is the same as for the previous mayonnaise except that, at the end, you add only 1 tablespoon of *fromage blanc* and you add if you have them on hand:

    1 heaping teaspoon of **carrot purée (137)**
    1 tablespoon of **onion purée (146)**

Fold in the beaten egg white at the very end, as before.

NOTE: *The possibilities for experimenting with vegetable purées in mayonnaise minceur are many. You need to remember that the purées must be cooked and that they must not contain excess liquid. Fresh herbs will blend better if they are first blanched in boiling water and minced. Ed.*

Sauce Créosat
COLD VEGETABLE SAUCE FOR GRILLED BEEF

To make 1 cup:

VEGETABLES:
5 tablespoons of diced cucumber
2 tablespoons of diced green pepper
¾ cup of diced onion
2 tablespoons of diced tomato, drained

SEASONINGS:
1 teaspoon of olive oil
3 tablespoons of red-wine vinegar
½ teaspoon Worcestershire
½ teaspoon of Dijon mustard
1 tablespoon of minced sour gherkins (*cornichons*)
1 scant tablespoon of pickled capers
1 whole clove of garlic, peeled and split
A sprig of thyme
½ bay leaf
Salt and pepper

The vegetables should all be cut into ¼-inch dice, or smaller. Combine them in a bowl. In another bowl, blend all the seasonings together with a fork, as for a *vinaigrette*. Add this sauce to the vegetables, mix well, and store in the refrigerator in a covered container to marinate at least 3 days before using.

Sauce grelette

TOMATO CREAM SAUCE FOR SALAD

To serve ten:

1 ¼ pounds of firm ripe tomatoes
6 tablespoons of **fromage blanc (173)**
1 tablespoon of **créme fraîche (172)**
1 teaspoon of finely minced parsley
½ teaspoon of finely minced tarragon
1 tablespoon of ketchup
2 teaspoons of armagnac or cognac (*optional*)
Lemon juice
2 teaspoons of salt
White pepper

Prepare the tomatoes as for raw **diced fresh tomatoes (130)**. Dice them not too coarsely, and drain. In a bowl, beat together with a whisk the *fromage blanc* and *crème fraîche*. Add the chopped herbs, ketchup, armagnac or cognac, and the lemon juice to taste, and whisk again. Then stir in the diced tomatoes, and season with the salt and a good pinch of white pepper. Store in a covered container in the refrigerator.

The sauce may be served from a bowl set in another bowl of cracked ice.

Sauce homardiere 1

COLD LOBSTER SAUCE

To make about 1 ½ cups:

> 1 recipe **low-calorie mayonnaise (32)**
> 4 tablespoons of **lobster sauce américaine (18)**
> A spoonful of vegetables, diced, from **court-bouillon (83)**
> ½ teaspoon of minced fresh tarragon
> ½ teaspoon of minced fresh chervil or parsley
>
> 1 egg white, reserved from making the mayonnaise
>
> UTENSILS:
> Little saucepan
> Bowl
> Small whisk

In the little saucepan, over low heat, simmer the *lobster sauce americaine* until it is reduced by about half, let cool, and chill in the refrigerator.

Make the mayonnaise, but do not add the egg white. Whisk in the *sauce américaine* and the minced herbs, and refrigerate, Shortly before serving, beat the egg white and fold it gently into the *sauce homardiére*. Depending on what you use this sauce with, the diced vegetables may be either sprinkled over the dish or stirred into the sauce when you add the sauce *américaine* and the herbs.

Sauce Vierge
MINCEUR TOMATO SAUCE

To serve four:

> Raw diced **fresh tomatoes (130)** made with 3 firm, ripe tomatoes
> 3 tablespoons of olive oil
> 4 level tablespoons of **fromage blanc** (173) (*optional*)
> 1 teaspoon of Dijon mustard
> 1 teaspoon of Worcestershire sauce
> 1 clove of garlic, unpeeled, crushed
> 2 tablespoons of minced fresh chervil
> 2 tablespoons of minced fresh parsley
> 1 tablespoon of minced fresh tarragon
> 8 coriander seeds, crushed in a mortar
> Salt and pepper

Starting with the olive oil, mix all the following ingredients except the salt and pepper together well with a fork, then add the diced tomatoes, and season to taste. This sauce is not cooked—it is only heated over hot water.

Sauce béarnaise Eugénie 1
LOW-CALORIE BÉARNAISE SAUCE

To serve eight:

AROMATIC MIXTURE FOR REDUCTION:
4 tablespoons of red-wine vinegar
6 tablespoons of finely minced shallot
1 teaspoon of crushed peppercorns (*poivre mignonnette*)
1 tablespoon of minced fresh tarragon
have ready to finish the sauce:
1½ cups of raw **diced fresh tomatoes (130)**, drained
1 tablespoon of **mushroom purée (136)**
1 teaspoon of minced fresh chervil or parsley

Salt to taste

LIAISON:
5 tablespoons of cold water, in all
2 egg yolks
2 tablespoons of olive oil

UTENSILS:
Two small enameled or stainless heavy-bottomed saucepans
Bowls for separating eggs
Whisk
Saucepan of warm, not boiling water (*bain marie*)

In the first saucepan combine the vinegar, shallot, pepper, and tarragon. Simmer over medium heat, uncovered, for about 5 minutes, or until the liquid is reduced by about three quarters; you should have a soft, juicy, but not liquid "marmalade" left. Allow this to cool and in the meantime separate the eggs and lightly whisk the yolks.

At the same time, in the second saucepan, simmer the diced raw tomatoes until all the excess liquid has evaporated.

Off the heat, add to the vinegar-shallot reduction 1 tablespoon of the cold water and, with the whisk, beat in the egg yolks. Put the saucepan back over low heat, and heat, whisking constantly, until the mixture thickens and becomes creamy. It must not heat past lukewarm (test with your finger), and it is thick enough when the movement of the whisk exposes streaks of the bottom of the pan.

Now, still whisking, add the olive oil and then, gradually, the remaining 4 tablespoons of cold water. Heat and whisk until the sauce has a good consistency, then stir in the simmered tomatoes, the mushroom purée, and the chervil. Taste for seasoning. Set the saucepan aside over warm water until you are ready to serve the sauce.

Sauce béarnaise Eugénie II
LOW-CALORIE BÉARNAISE SAUCE WITH STOCK

To serve eight:

AROMATIC MIXTURE FOR REDUCTION:
4 tablespoons of red-wine vinegar
6 tablespoons of finely minced shallot
1 teaspoon of crushed peppercorns (*poivre mignonnette*)
1 tablespoon of minced fresh tarragon

HAVE READY TO FINISH THE SAUCE:

1½ cups of raw **diced fresh tomatoes (130)**, drained

1 teaspoon of tomato paste

1 teaspoon of minced fresh chervil or parsley

Salt to taste

LIAISON:

1 tablespoon of cold water

2 egg yolks

2 tablespoons of olive oil

½ cup of hot **chicken stock (5)** (*see Note*)

UTENSILS:

Two small enameled or stainless heavy-bottomed saucepans

Bowls for separating eggs

Whisk

Saucepan of warm, not boiling water (*bain marie*)

NOTE: *For this sauce, you should use real homemade stock, which has the gelatin content lacking in canned or bouillon-cube broths, Ed.*

In the first saucepan combine the vinegar, shallot, pepper, and tarragon. Simmer over medium heat, uncovered, for about 5 minutes, or until the liquid is reduced by about three quarters; you should have a soft, juicy, but not liquid "marmalade" left. Allow this to cool and in the meantime separate the eggs and lightly whisk the yolks.

At the same time, in the second saucepan, simmer the diced raw tomatoes until all the excess liquid has evaporated.

Off the heat, add to the vinegar-shallot reduction the tablespoon of cold water and, with the whisk, beat in the egg yolks. Put the saucepan back over low heat, and heat, whisking constantly, until the mixture thickens and becomes creamy. It must not heat past lukewarm (test with your finger), and it is thick enough when the movement of the whisk exposes streaks of the bottom of the pan.

Now, still whisking, add the olive oil and then, gradually, the hot chicken stock. Heat and whisk until the sauce has a good consistency, then stir in the simmered tomatoes, the tomato paste, and the chervil. Taste for seasoning. Set the saucepan aside over warm water until you are ready to serve the sauce.

Sauce beurre blanc minceur

LOW-CALORIE FOAMY BUTTER SAUCE

To serve four:

¼ cup of dry white wine
¼ cup of white-wine vinegar
2 tablespoons of finely minced shallot
4 tablespoons (½ stick) of cold butter, in one piece; the butter must come straight from the refrigerator
1 teaspoon of **crème fraîche (172)**
½ cup of **fromage blanc (173)**
Salt and pepper

UTENSILS:
Small enameled or stainless heavy-bottomed saucepan
Small whisk

In the saucepan combine the wine, vinegar, and shallot, and simmer over medium heat, uncovered, until the liquid has reduced by about two thirds, or to just under 3 tablespoons. (*To see in advance how this will look, put 3 tablespoons of water in the saucepan before you make the sauce; the whole bottom of the pan should be covered with a shallow puddle. Ed.*)

Then: Have the reduced liquid boiling briskly over direct heat. Put the piece of cold butter in the middle of the pan and add the teaspoon of *crème fraîche.* The butter will melt, of course, and as it does, the bubbling liquid will absorb it and lightly thicken it simultaneously; the cream helps this process as well. Stir only when the butter is more than half melted, and when it is all melted set the pan aside to cool to lukewarm.

Now whisk in the *fromage blanc* and taste for seasoning. (*You may reheat the sauce very gently over hot water, but not for long. Ed.*)

Sauce coulis de tomates fraîches

FRESH TOMATO PURÉE SAUCE

Served hot or cold. To make 1 quart:

2 pounds firm, ripe tomatoes, peeled
1 tablespoon of olive oil
3 shallots, peeled and chopped
1 clove of garlic, unpeeled, crushed
1 tablespoon of tomato paste

Bouquet garni
2 ¼ cups of **chicken stock (5) (8)**
Salt and pepper

UTENSILS:
Kettle of boiling water
Bowl of ice water
Heavy-bottomed stainless saucepan
Electric blender

To peel the tomatoes, plunge them into boiling water for 15 seconds and then plunge them into cold water so that the tomato just under the skin will not begin to cook. (*An easy way to do this is to put the tomatoes on a rack in the kitchen sink, stem ends up. Pour boiling water over them, which goes quickly down the drain. Turn the tomatoes over, pour boiling water over them again, and transfer them to the bowl of ice water. Ed.*) They are now very easy to peel. After peeling, cut the tomatoes in half crosswise, and gently squeeze them in the palm of your hand to eliminate the seeds and excess juice.

Heat the olive oil in the saucepan and in it gently cook the shallots. Add the garlic, tomatoes, tomato paste, *bouquet garni,* and chicken stock. Simmer over moderate heat for 20 minutes.

Remove the *bouquet garni,* purée the tomato sauce in the electric blender, and season it lightly to taste with salt and pepper. If the sauce is too thin, pour it back into the saucepan and simmer it again until it is reduced to a good but not heavy consistency.

Sauce coulis d' asperges
ASPARAGUS PURÉE SAUCE

To serve four or more:

¾ pound of fresh green or white asparagus, or 10½-ounce can of white asparagus
½ cup of **chicken stock (5) (8)**
1 teaspoon of salt
A pinch of pepper
1 teaspoon of **crème fraîche (172)** (*optional*)

UTENSILS:
Asparagus cooker
Electric blender
Small enameled or stainless saucepan or double boiler

If you are using fresh green or white asparagus, cook them according to the instructions on page 50. Or, heat the canned asparagus in their own juice and drain them. Cut the asparagus into 1-inch pieces (discard any stringy parts that may remain at the bases), and purée them in the electric blender with the chicken stock, salt and pepper, and cream. Taste for seasoning and keep warm over hot water.

Sauce coulis d' artichauts

ARTICHOKE PURÉE SAUCE

To serve four or five:

3 small artichokes, or 1½ to 1¾ pounds in all
2 quarts of water
2 tablespoons of coarse salt
Juice of 1 lemon
½ cup **chicken stock (5) (8)**
1 teaspoon of **crème fraîche (172)**
Salt and pepper

UTENSILS:
Enameled or stainless kettle with a lid
Electric blender
Small enameled or stainless saucepan or double boiler

Wash the artichokes, cut off the stems, and cook the artichokes, covered, for 45 minutes in boiling salted water acidulated with the lemon juice. Put them in cold water to cool.

Remove all the leaves and scoop out the chokes. Cut the artichoke bottoms in pieces and purée them in the electric blender with the chicken stock and cream. Taste for seasoning and keep arm over hot water.

Sauce au persil

PARSLEY SAUCE

To serve four:

A large bunch of parsley, preferably the flat Italian variety
2 shallots, peeled and finely minced
1 cup of stock (see Note)
2 teaspoons of **mushroom purée** (136)
2 tablespoons of **fromage blanc** (173)
Lemon juice
Salt and pepper

UTENSILS:
Enameled or stainless saucepan
Strainer
Electric blender

NOTE: *To serve with meat, use* **veal stock (1) (4)**; *to serve with seafood, use* **fish stock (9) (11)**. *Ed.*

Remove all the stems from the parsley and use only the leaves. In the saucepan, cook together over low heat the parsley, shallots, and stock for 15 minutes. Strain the mixture and reserve the stock. Put the parsley and shallots in the electric blender and add the mushroom purée, *fromage blanc*, and a squeeze of lemon juice. Blend well, and thin the purée with some of the stock. Taste for seasoning and keep the sauce warm.

Sauce à la crème d'ail

GARLIC CREAM SAUCE

To serve four:

12 cloves of garlic, peeled
1½ cups of water
3 medium-size mushrooms, stems trimmed, rinsed, and cut in half
½ teaspoon of salt
A pinch of nutmeg
½ cup of nonfat dry milk
1 teaspoon of **glace de viande (3)**
2 teaspoons of chopped parsley
Squeeze of lemon juice (*optional*)

UTENSILS:
Saucepan
Small heavy-bottomed saucepan
Electric blender

In the saucepan, blanch the garlic in unsalted boiling water three times, changing the water each time. In the heavy-bottomed saucepan, combine the 1½ *cups of water and the garlic, mushrooms, salt, and nutmeg. Simmer all together, covered, over low heat for 15 minutes. Then stir in the dry milk, and simmer for another 5 minutes.*

Add the *glace de viande* and parsley, and purée the sauce in the electric blender. Then add the lemon juice, taste for seasoning, and keep warm.

OUT OF THE KITCHEN, ONTO THE COUCH

By Michael Pollan

1. JULIA'S CHILDREN

I was only 8 when "The French Chef" first appeared on American television in 1963, but it didn't take long for me to realize that this Julia Child had improved the quality of life around our house. My mother began cooking dishes she'd watched Julia cook on TV: boeuf bourguignon (the subject of the show's first episode), French onion soup gratinée, duck à l'orange, coq au vin, mousse au chocolat. Some of the more ambitious dishes, like the duck or the mousse, were pointed toward weekend company, but my mother would usually test these out on me and my sisters earlier in the week, and a few of the others—including the boeuf bourguignon, which I especially loved—actually made it into heavy weeknight rotation. So whenever people talk about how Julia Child upgraded the culture of food in America, I nod appreciatively. I owe her. Not that I didn't also owe Swanson, because we also ate TV dinners, and those were pretty good, too.

Every so often I would watch "The French Chef" with my mother in the den. On WNET in New York, it came on late in the afternoon, after school, and because we had only one television back then, if Mom wanted to watch her program, you watched it, too. The show felt less like TV than like hanging around the kitchen, which is to say, not terribly exciting to a kid (except when Child dropped something on the floor, which my mother promised would happen if we stuck around long enough) but comforting in its familiarity: the clanking of pots and pans, the squeal of an oven door in need of WD-40, all the kitchen-chemistry-set spectacles of transformation. The show was taped live and broadcast uncut and unedited, so it had a vérité feel completely unlike anything you might see today on the Food Network, with its A.D.H.D. editing and hyperkinetic soundtracks of rock music and clashing knives. While Julia waited for the butter foam to subside in the sauté pan, you waited, too, precisely as long, listening to Julia's improvised patter over the hiss of her pan, as she filled the desultory minutes with kitchen tips and lore. It all felt more like life than TV, though Julia's voice was like nothing I ever heard before or would hear again until Monty Python came to America: vaguely European, breathy and singsongy, and weirdly suggestive of a man doing a falsetto impression of a woman. The BBC supposedly took "The French Chef" off the air because viewers wrote in complaining that Julia Child seemed either drunk or demented.

Meryl Streep, who brings Julia Child vividly back to the screen in Nora Ephron's charming new comedy, "Julie & Julia," has the voice down, and with the help of some clever set design and cinematography, she manages to evoke too Child's big-girl ungainliness—the woman was 6 foot 2 and had arms like a longshoreman. Streep also captures the deep sensual delight that Julia Child took in food—not just the eating of it (her virgin bite of sole meunière at La Couronne in Rouen recalls Meg Ryan's deli orgasm in "When Harry Met Sally") but the fondling and affectionate slapping of ingredients in their raw state and the magic of their kitchen transformations.

But "Julie & Julia" is more than an exercise in nostalgia. As the title suggests, the film has a second, more contemporary heroine. The Julie character (played by Amy Adams) is based on Julie Powell, a 29-year-old aspiring writer living in Queens who, casting about for a blog conceit in 2002, hit on a cool one: she would cook her way through all 524 recipes in Child's "Mastering the Art of French Cooking" in 365 days and blog about her adventures. The movie shuttles back and forth between Julie's year of compulsive cooking and blogging in Queens in 2002 and Julia's decade in Paris and Provence a half-century earlier, as recounted in "My Life in France," the memoir published a few years after her death in 2004. Julia Child in 1949 was in some ways in the same boat in which Julie Powell found herself in 2002: happily married to a really nice guy but feeling, acutely, the lack of a life project. Living in Paris, where her husband, Paul Child, was posted in the diplomatic corps, Julia (who like Julie had worked as a secretary) was at a loss as to what to do with her life until she realized that what she liked to do best was eat. So she enrolled in Le Cordon Bleu and learned how to cook. As with Julia, so with Julie: cooking saved her life, giving her a project and, eventually, a path to literary success.

That learning to cook could lead an American woman to success of any kind would have seemed utterly implausible in 1949; that it is so thoroughly plausible 60 years later owes everything to Julia Child's legacy. Julie Powell operates in a world that Julia Child helped to create, one where food is taken seriously, where chefs have been welcomed into the repertory company of American celebrity and where cooking has become a broadly appealing mise-en-scène in which success stories can plausibly be set and played out. How amazing is it that we live today in a culture that has not only something called the Food Network but now a hit show on that network called "The Next Food Network Star," which thousands of 20- and 30-somethings compete eagerly to become? It would seem we have come a long way from Swanson TV dinners.

The Food Network can now be seen in nearly 100 million American homes and on most nights commands more viewers than any of the cable news channels. Millions of

Americans, including my 16-year-old son, can tell you months after the finale which contestant emerged victorious in Season 5 of "Top Chef" (Hosea Rosenberg, followed by Stefan Richter, his favorite, and Carla Hall). The popularity of cooking shows—or perhaps I should say food shows—has spread beyond the precincts of public or cable television to the broadcast networks, where Gordon Ramsay terrorizes newbie chefs on "Hell's Kitchen" on Fox and Jamie Oliver is preparing a reality show on ABC in which he takes aim at an American city with an obesity problem and tries to teach the population how to cook. It's no wonder that a Hollywood studio would conclude that American audiences had an appetite for a movie in which the road to personal fulfillment and public success passes through the kitchen and turns, crucially, on a recipe for boeuf bourguignon. (The secret is to pat dry your beef before you brown it.)

But here's what I don't get: How is it that we are so eager to watch other people browning beef cubes on screen but so much less eager to brown them ourselves? For the rise of Julia Child as a figure of cultural consequence—along with Alice Waters and Mario Batali and Martha Stewart and Emeril Lagasse and whoever is crowned the next Food Network star—has, paradoxically, coincided with the rise of fast food, home-meal replacements and the decline and fall of everyday home cooking.

That decline has several causes: women working outside the home; food companies persuading Americans to let them do the cooking; and advances in technology that made it easier for them to do so. Cooking is no longer obligatory, and for many people, women especially, that has been a blessing. But perhaps a mixed blessing, to judge by the culture's continuing, if not deepening, fascination with the subject. It has been easier for us to give up cooking than it has been to give up talking about it—and watching it.

Today the average American spends a mere 27 minutes a day on food preparation (another four minutes cleaning up); that's less than half the time that we spent cooking and cleaning up when Julia arrived on our television screens. It's also less than half the time it takes to watch a single episode of "Top Chef" or "Chopped" or "The Next Food Network Star." What this suggests is that a great many Americans are spending considerably more time watching images of cooking on television than they are cooking themselves—an increasingly archaic activity they will tell you they no longer have the time for.

What is wrong with this picture?

2. THE COURAGE TO FLIP

When I asked my mother recently what exactly endeared Julia Child to her, she explained that "for so many of us she took the fear out of cooking" and, to illustrate the point, brought up the famous potato show (or, as Julia pronounced it, "the poh-TAY-toh show!"), one of the episodes that Meryl Streep recreates brilliantly on screen. Millions of Americans of a certain age claim to remember Julia Child dropping a chicken or a goose on the floor, but the memory is apocryphal: what she dropped was a potato pancake, and it didn't quite make it to the floor. Still, this was a classic live-television moment, inconceivable on any modern cooking show: Martha Stewart would sooner commit seppuku than let such an outtake ever see the light of day.

The episode has Julia making a plate-size potato pancake, sautéing a big disc of mashed potato into which she has folded impressive quantities of cream and butter. Then the fateful moment arrives:

"When you flip anything, you just have to have the courage of your convictions," she declares, clearly a tad nervous at the prospect, and then gives the big pancake a flip. On the way down, half of it catches the lip of the pan and splats onto the stovetop. Undaunted, Julia scoops the thing up and roughly patches the pancake back together, explaining: "When I flipped it, I didn't have the courage to do it the way I should have. You can always pick it up." And then, looking right through the camera as if taking us into her confidence, she utters the line that did so much to lift the fear of failure from my mother and her contemporaries: "If you're alone in the kitchen, WHOOOO"—the pronoun is sung—"is going to see?" For a generation of women eager to transcend their mothers' recipe box (and perhaps, too, their mothers' social standing), Julia's little kitchen catastrophe was a liberation and a lesson: "The only way you learn to flip things is just to flip them!"

It was a kind of courage—not only to cook but to cook the world's most glamorous and intimidating cuisine—that Julia Child gave my mother and so many other women like her, and to watch her empower viewers in episode after episode is to appreciate just how much about cooking on television—not to mention cooking itself—has changed in the years since "The French Chef" was on the air.

There are still cooking programs that will teach you how to cook. Public television offers the eminently useful "America's Test Kitchen." The Food Network carries a whole slate of so-called dump-and-stir shows during the day, and the network's research suggests that at least some viewers are following along. But many of these programs—I'm thinking of Rachael Ray, Paula Deen, Sandra Lee—tend to be aimed at stay-at-home moms who are in a hurry and eager to please. ("How good are you going to look when you serve this?" asks Paula Deen, a Southern gal of the old school.) These shows stress quick results, shortcuts and superconvenience but never the sort of pleasure—physical and mental—that Julia Child took in the work of cooking: the tomahawking of a fish skeleton or the chopping of an onion, the Rolfing of butter into the breast of a raw chicken or the vigorous whisking of heavy cream. By the end of the potato show, Julia was out of breath and had broken a sweat, which she mopped from her brow with a paper towel. (Have you ever seen Martha Stewart break a sweat? Pant? If so, you know her a lot better than the rest of us.) Child was less interested in making it fast or easy than making it right, because cooking for her was so much more than a means to a meal. It was a gratifying, even ennobling sort of work, engaging both the mind and the muscles. You didn't do it to please a husband or impress guests; you did it to please yourself. No one cooking on television today gives the impression that they enjoy the actual work quite as much as Julia Child did. In this, she strikes me as a more liberated figure than many of the women who have followed her on television.

Curiously, the year Julia Child went on the air—1963—was the same year Betty Friedan published "The Feminine Mystique," the book that taught millions of American women to regard housework, cooking included, as drudgery, indeed as a form of oppression. You may think of these two figures as antagonists, but that wouldn't be quite right. They actually had a great deal in common, as Child's biographer, Laura Shapiro, points out, and addressed the aspirations of many of the same women. Julia never referred to her viewers as "housewives"—a word she detested—and never condescended to them. She tried to show the sort of women who read "The Feminine Mystique" that, far from oppressing them, the work of cooking approached in the proper spirit offered a kind of fulfillment and deserved an intelligent woman's attention. (A man's too.) Second-wave feminists were often ambivalent on the gender politics of cooking. Simone de Beauvoir wrote in "The Second Sex" that though cooking could be oppressive, it could also be a form of "revelation and creation; and a woman can find special satisfaction in a successful cake or a flaky pastry, for not everyone can do it: one must have the gift." This can be read either as a special Frenchie exemption for the culinary arts (féminisme, c'est bon, but we must not jeopardize those flaky pastries!) or as a bit of wisdom that some American feminists thoughtlessly trampled in their rush to get women out of the kitchen.

3. TO THE KITCHEN STADIUM

Whichever, kitchen work itself has changed considerably since 1963, judging from its depiction on today's how-to shows. Take the concept of cooking from scratch. Many of today's cooking programs rely unapologetically on ingredients that themselves contain lots of ingredients: canned soups, jarred mayonnaise, frozen vegetables, powdered sauces, vanilla wafers, limeade concentrate, Marshmallow Fluff. This probably shouldn't surprise us: processed foods have so thoroughly colonized the American kitchen and diet that they have redefined what passes today for cooking, not to mention food. Many of these convenience foods have been sold to women as tools of liberation; the rhetoric of kitchen oppression has been cleverly hijacked by food marketers and the cooking shows they sponsor to sell more stuff. So the shows encourage home cooks to take all manner of shortcuts, each of which involves buying another product, and all of which taken together have succeeded in redefining what is commonly meant by the verb "to cook."

I spent an enlightening if somewhat depressing hour on the phone with a veteran food-marketing researcher, Harry Balzer, who explained that "people call things 'cooking' today that would roll their grandmother in her grave—heating up a can of soup or microwaving a frozen pizza." Balzer has been studying American eating habits since 1978; the NPD Group, the firm he works for, collects data from a pool of 2,000 food diaries to track American eating habits. Years ago Balzer noticed that the definition of cooking held by his respondents had grown so broad as to be meaningless, so the firm tightened up the meaning of "to cook" at least slightly to capture what was really going on in American kitchens. To cook from scratch, they decreed, means to prepare a main dish that requires some degree of "assembly of elements." So microwaving a pizza doesn't count as cooking, though washing a head of lettuce and pouring bottled dressing over it does. Under this dispensation, you're also cooking when you spread mayonnaise on a slice of bread and pile on some cold cuts or a hamburger patty. (Currently the most popular meal in America, at both lunch and dinner, is a sandwich; the No. 1 accompanying beverage is a soda.) At least by Balzer's none-too-exacting standard, Americans are still cooking up a storm—58 percent of our evening meals qualify, though even that figure has been falling steadily since the 1980s.

Like most people who study consumer behavior, Balzer has developed a somewhat cynical view of human nature, which his research suggests is ever driven by the quest to save time or money or, optimally, both. I kept asking him what his research had to say about the prevalence of the activity I referred to as "real scratch cooking," but he wouldn't touch the term. Why? Apparently the activity has become so rarefied as to elude his tools of measurement.

"Here's an analogy," Balzer said. "A hundred years ago, chicken for dinner meant going out and catching, killing, plucking and gutting a chicken. Do you know anybody who still does that? It would be considered crazy! Well, that's exactly how cooking will seem to your grandchildren: something people used to do when they had no other choice. Get over it."

After my discouraging hour on the phone with Balzer, I settled in for a couple more with the Food Network, trying to square his dismal view of our interest in cooking with the hyperexuberant, even fetishized images of cooking that are presented on the screen. The Food Network undergoes a complete change of personality at night, when it trades the cozy precincts of the home kitchen and chirpy softball coaching of Rachael Ray or Sandra Lee for something markedly less feminine and less practical. Erica Gruen, the cable executive often credited with putting the Food Network on the map in the late '90s, recognized early on that, as she told a journalist, "people don't watch television to learn things." So she shifted the network's target audience from people who love to cook to people who love to eat, a considerably larger universe and one that—important for a cable network—happens to contain a great many more men.

In prime time, the Food Network's mise-en-scène shifts to masculine arenas like the Kitchen Stadium on "Iron Chef," where famous restaurant chefs wage gladiatorial combat to see who can, in 60 minutes, concoct the most spectacular meal from a secret ingredient ceremoniously unveiled just as the clock starts: an octopus or a bunch of bananas or a whole school of daurade. Whether in the Kitchen Stadium or on "Chopped" or "The Next Food Network Star" or, over on Bravo, "Top Chef," cooking in prime time is a form of athletic competition, drawing its visual and even aural vocabulary from "Monday Night Football." On "Iron Chef America," one of the Food Network's biggest hits, the cookingcaster Alton Brown delivers a breathless (though always gently tongue-in-cheek) play by play and color commentary, as the iron chefs and their team of iron sous-chefs race the clock to peel, chop, slice, dice, mince, Cuisinart, mandoline, boil, double-boil, pan-sear, sauté, sous vide, deep-fry, pressure-cook, grill, deglaze, reduce, and plate—this last a word I'm old enough to remember when it was a mere noun. A particularly dazzling display of chefly "knife skills"—a term bandied as freely on the Food Network as "passing game" or "slugging percentage" is on ESPN—will earn an instant replay: an onion minced in slo-mo. Can we get a camera on this, Alton Brown will ask in a hushed, this-must-be-golf tone of voice. It looks like Chef Flay's going to try for a last-minute garnish grab before the clock runs out! Will he make it? [The buzzer sounds.] Yes!

These shows move so fast, in such a blur of flashing knives, frantic pantry raids and more sheer fire than you would ever want to see in your own kitchen, that I honestly can't tell you whether that "last-minute garnish grab" happened on "Iron Chef America" or "Chopped" or "The Next Food Network Star" or whether it was Chef Flay or Chef Batali who snagged the sprig of foliage at the buzzer. But impressive it surely was, in the same way it's impressive to watch a handful of eager young chefs on "Chopped" figure out how to make a passable appetizer from chicken wings, celery, soba noodles and a package of string cheese in just 20 minutes, said starter to be judged by a panel of professional chefs on the basis of "taste, creativity and presentation." (If you ask me, the key to victory on any of these shows comes down to one factor: bacon. Whichever contestant puts bacon in the dish invariably seems to win.)

But you do have to wonder how easily so specialized a set of skills might translate to the home kitchen—or anywhere else for that matter. For when in real life are even professional chefs required to conceive and execute dishes in 20 minutes from ingredients selected by a third party exhibiting obvious sadistic tendencies? (String cheese?) Never, is when. The skills celebrated on the Food Network in prime time are precisely the skills necessary to succeed on the Food Network in prime time. They will come in handy nowhere else on God's green earth.

We learn things watching these cooking competitions, but they're not things about how to cook. There are no recipes to follow; the contests fly by much too fast for viewers to take in any practical tips; and the kind of cooking practiced in prime time is far more spectacular than anything you would ever try at home. No, for anyone hoping to pick up a few dinnertime tips, the implicit message of today's prime-time cooking shows is, Don't try this at home. If you really want to eat this way, go to a restaurant. Or as a chef friend put it when I asked him if he thought I could learn anything about cooking by watching the Food Network, "How much do you learn about playing basketball by watching the N.B.A.?"

What we mainly learn about on the Food Network in prime time is culinary fashion, which is no small thing: if Julia took the fear out of cooking, these shows take the fear—the social anxiety—out of ordering in restaurants. (Hey, now I know what a shiso leaf is and what "crudo" means!) Then, at the judges' table, we learn how to taste and how to talk about food. For viewers, these shows have become less about the production of high-end food than about its consumption—including its conspicuous consumption. (I think I'll start with the sawfish crudo wrapped in shiso leaves. …)

Surely it's no accident that so many Food Network stars have themselves found a way to transcend barriers of social class in the kitchen—beginning with Emeril Lagasse, the working-class guy from Fall River, Mass., who, though he may not be able to sound the 'r' in "garlic," can still cook like a dream. Once upon a time Julia made the same promise in reverse: she showed you how you, too, could cook like someone who could not only prepare but properly pronounce a béarnaise. So-called fancy food has always served as a form of cultural capital, and cooking programs help you acquire it, now without so much as lifting a spatula. The glamour of food has made it something of a class leveler in America, a fact that many of these shows implicitly celebrate. Television likes nothing better than to serve up elitism to the masses, paradoxical as that might sound. How wonderful is it that something like arugula can at the same time be a mark of sophistication and be found in almost every salad bar in America? Everybody wins!

But the shift from producing food on television to consuming it strikes me as a far-less-salubrious development. Traditionally, the recipe for the typical dump-and-stir program comprises about 80 percent cooking followed by 20 percent eating, but in prime time you now find a raft of shows that flip that ratio on its head, like "The Best Thing I Ever Ate" and "Diners, Drive-Ins and Dives," which are about nothing but eating. Sure, Guy Fieri, the tattooed and spiky-coiffed chowhound who hosts "Diners, Drive-Ins and Dives," ducks into the kitchen whenever he visits one of these roadside joints to do a little speed-bonding with the startled short-order cooks in back, but most of the time he's wrapping his mouth around their supersize creations: a 16-ounce Oh Gawd! burger (with the works); battered and deep-fried anything (clams, pickles, cinnamon buns, stuffed peppers, you name it); or a buttermilk burrito approximately the size of his head, stuffed with bacon, eggs, and cheese. What Fieri's critical vocabulary lacks in analytical rigor, it more than makes up for in tailgate enthusiasm: "Man, oh man, now this is what I'm talkin' about!" What can possibly be the appeal of watching Guy Fieri bite, masticate and swallow all this chow?

The historical drift of cooking programs—from a genuine interest in producing food yourself to the spectacle of merely consuming it—surely owes a lot to the decline of cooking in our culture, but it also has something to do with the gravitational field that eventually overtakes anything in television's orbit. It's no accident that Julia Child appeared on public television—or educational television, as it used to be called. On a commercial network, a program that actually inspired viewers to get off the couch and spend an hour cooking a meal would be a commercial disaster, for it would mean they were turning off the television to do something else. The ads on the Food Network, at least in prime time, strongly suggest its viewers do no such thing: the food-related ads hardly ever hawk kitchen appliances or ingredients (unless you count A.1. steak sauce) but rather push the usual supermarket cart of edible foodlike substances, including Manwich sloppy joe in a can, Special K protein shakes, and Ore-Ida frozen French fries, along with fast-casual eateries like Olive Garden and Red Lobster.

Buying, not making, is what cooking shows are mostly now about—that and, increasingly, cooking shows themselves: the whole self-perpetuating spectacle of competition, success and celebrity that, with "The Next Food Network Star," appears to have entered its baroque phase. The Food Network has figured out that we care much less about what's cooking than who's cooking. A few years ago, Mario Batali neatly summed up the network's formula to a reporter: "Look, it's TV! Everyone has to fall into a niche. I'm the Italian guy. Emeril's the exuberant New Orleans guy with the big eyebrows who yells a lot. Bobby's the grilling guy. Rachael Ray is the cheerleader-type girl who makes things at home the way a regular person would. Giada's the beautiful girl with the nice rack who does simple Italian food. As silly as the whole Food Network is, it gives us all a soapbox to talk about the things we care about." Not to mention a platform from which to sell all their stuff.

The Food Network has helped to transform cooking from something you do into something you watch—into yet another confection of spectacle and celebrity that keeps us pinned to the couch. The formula is as circular and self-reinforcing as a TV dinner: a simulacrum of home cooking that is sold on TV and designed to be eaten in front of the TV. True, in the case of the Swanson rendition, at least you get something that will fill you up; by comparison, the Food Network leaves you hungry, a condition its advertisers must love. But in neither case is there much risk that you will get off the couch and actually cook a meal. Both kinds of TV dinner plant us exactly where television always wants us: in front of the set, watching.

4. WATCHING WHAT WE EAT

To point out that television has succeeded in turning cooking into a spectator sport raises the question of why anyone would want to watch other people cook in the first place. There are plenty of things we've stopped doing for ourselves that we have no desire to watch other people do on TV: you don't see shows about changing the oil in your car or ironing shirts or reading newspapers. So what is it about cooking, specifically, that makes it such good television just now?

It's worth keeping in mind that watching other people cook is not exactly a new behavior for us humans. Even when "everyone" still cooked, there were plenty of us who mainly watched: men, for the most part, and children. Most of us have happy memories of watching our mothers in the kitchen, performing feats that sometimes looked very much like sorcery and typically resulted in something tasty to eat. Watching my mother transform the raw materials of nature—a handful of plants, an animal's flesh—into a favorite dinner was always a pretty good show, but on the afternoons when she tackled a complex marvel like chicken Kiev, I happily stopped whatever I was doing to watch. (I told you we had it pretty good, thanks partly to Julia.) My mother would hammer the boneless chicken breasts into flat pink slabs, roll them tightly around chunks of ice-cold herbed butter, glue the cylinders shut with egg, then fry the little logs until they turned golden brown, in what qualified as a minor miracle of transubstantiation. When the dish turned out right, knifing through the crust into the snowy white meat within would uncork a fragrant ooze of melted butter that seeped across the plate to merge with the Minute Rice. (If the instant rice sounds all wrong, remember that in the 1960s, Julia Child and modern food science were both tokens of sophistication.)

Yet even the most ordinary dish follows a similar arc of transformation, magically becoming something greater than the sum of its parts. Every dish contains not just culinary ingredients but also the ingredients of narrative: a beginning, a middle, and an end. Bring in the element of fire—cooking's deus ex machina—and you've got a tasty little drama right there, the whole thing unfolding in a TV-friendly span of time: 30 minutes (at 350 degrees) will usually do it.

Cooking shows also benefit from the fact that food itself is—by definition—attractive to the humans who eat it, and that attraction can be enhanced by food styling, an art at which the Food Network so excels as to make Julia Child look like a piker. You'll be flipping aimlessly through the cable channels when a slow-motion cascade of glistening red cherries or a tongue of flame lapping at a slab of meat on the grill will catch your eye, and your reptilian brain will paralyze your thumb on the remote, forcing you to stop to see what's cooking. Food shows are the campfires in the deep cable forest, drawing us like hungry wanderers to their flames. (And on the Food Network there are plenty of flames to catch your eye, compensating, no doubt, for the unfortunate absence of aromas.)

No matter how well produced, a televised oil change and lube offers no such satisfactions.

I suspect we're drawn to the textures and rhythms of kitchen work, too, which seem so much more direct and satisfying than the more abstract and formless tasks most of us perform in our jobs nowadays. The chefs on TV get to put their hands on real stuff, not keyboards and screens but fundamental things like plants and animals and fungi; they get to work with fire and ice and perform feats of alchemy. By way of explaining why in the world she wants to cook her way through "Mastering the Art of French Cooking," all Julie Powell has to do in the film is show us her cubicle at the Lower Manhattan Development Corporation, where she spends her days on the phone mollifying callers with problems that she lacks the power to fix.

"You know what I love about cooking?" Julie tells us in a voice-over as we watch her field yet another inconclusive call on her headset. "I love that after a day where nothing is sure—and when I say nothing, I mean nothing—you can come home and absolutely know that if you add egg yolks to chocolate and sugar and milk, it will get thick. It's such a comfort." How many of us still do work that engages us in a dialogue with the material world and ends—assuming the soufflé doesn't collapse—with such a gratifying and tasty sense of closure? Come to think of it, even the collapse of the soufflé is at least definitive, which is more than you can say about most of what you will do at work tomorrow.

If cooking really offers all these satisfactions, then why don't we do more of it? Well, ask Julie Powell: for most of us it doesn't pay the rent, and very often our work doesn't leave us the time; during the year of Julia, dinner at the Powell apartment seldom arrived at the table before 10 p.m. For many years now, Americans have been putting in longer hours at work and enjoying less time at home. Since 1967, we've added 167 hours—the equivalent of a month's full-time labor—to the total amount of time we spend at work each year, and in households where both parents work, the figure is more like 400 hours. Americans today spend more time working than people in any other industrialized nation—an extra two weeks or more a year. Not surprisingly, in those countries where people still take cooking seriously, they also have more time to devote to it.

It's generally assumed that the entrance of women into the work force is responsible for the collapse of home cooking, but that turns out to be only part of the story. Yes, women with jobs outside the home spend less time cooking—but so do women without jobs. The amount of time spent on food preparation in America has fallen at the same precipitous rate among women who don't work outside the home as it has among women who do: in both cases, a decline of about 40 percent since 1965. (Though for married women who don't have jobs, the amount of time spent cooking remains greater: 58 minutes a day, as compared with 36 for married women who do have jobs.) In general, spending on restaurants or takeout food rises with income. Women with jobs have more money to pay corporations to do their cooking, yet all American women now allow corporations to cook for them when they can.

Those corporations have been trying to persuade Americans to let them do the cooking since long before large numbers of women entered the work force. After World War II, the food industry labored mightily to sell American women on all the processed-food wonders it had invented to feed the troops: canned meals, freeze-dried foods, dehydrated potatoes, powdered orange juice and coffee, instant everything. As Laura Shapiro recounts in "Something From the Oven: Reinventing Dinner in 1950s America," the food industry strived to "persuade millions of Americans to develop a lasting taste for meals that were a lot like field rations." The same process of peacetime conversion that industrialized our farming, giving us synthetic fertilizers made from munitions and new pesticides developed from nerve gas, also industrialized our eating.

Shapiro shows that the shift toward industrial cookery began not in response to a demand from women entering the work force but as a supply-driven phenomenon. In fact, for many years American women, whether they worked or not, resisted processed foods, regarding them as a dereliction of their "moral obligation to cook," something they believed to be a parental responsibility on par with child care. It took years of clever, dedicated marketing to break down this resistance and persuade Americans that opening a can or cooking from a mix really was cooking. Honest. In the 1950s, just-add-water cake mixes languished in the supermarket until the marketers figured out that if you left at least something for the "baker" to do—specifically, crack open an egg—she could take ownership of the cake. Over the years, the food scientists have gotten better and better at simulating real food, keeping it looking attractive and seemingly fresh, and the rapid acceptance of microwave ovens—which went from being in only 8 percent of American households in 1978 to 90 percent today—opened up vast new horizons of home-meal replacement.

Harry Balzer's research suggests that the corporate project of redefining what it means to cook and serve a meal has succeeded beyond the industry's wildest expectations. People think nothing of buying frozen peanut butter-and-jelly sandwiches for their children's lunchboxes. (Now how much of a timesaver can that be?) "We've had a hundred years of packaged foods," Balzer told me, "and now we're going to have a hundred years of packaged meals." Already today, 80 percent of the cost of food eaten in the home goes to someone other than a farmer, which is to say to industrial cooking and packaging and marketing. Balzer is unsentimental about this development: "Do you miss sewing or darning socks? I don't think so."

So what are we doing with the time we save by outsourcing our food preparation to corporations and 16-year-old burger flippers? Working, commuting to work, surfing the Internet and, perhaps most curiously of all, watching other people cook on television.

But this may not be quite the paradox it seems. Maybe the reason we like to watch cooking on TV is that there are things about cooking we miss. We might not feel we have the time or the energy to do it ourselves every day, yet we're not prepared to see it disappear from our lives entirely. Why? Perhaps because cooking—unlike sewing or darning socks—is an activity that strikes a deep emotional chord in us, one that might even go to the heart of our identity as human beings.

What?! You're telling me Bobby Flay strikes deep emotional chords?

Bear with me. Consider for a moment the proposition that as a human activity, cooking is far more important—to our happiness and to our health—than its current role in our lives, not to mention its depiction on TV, might lead you to believe. Let's see what happens when we take cooking seriously.

6. THE COOKING ANIMAL

The idea that cooking is a defining human activity is not a new one. In 1773, the Scottish writer James Boswell, noting that "no beast is a cook," called Homo sapiens "the cooking animal," though he might have reconsidered that definition had he been able to gaze upon the frozen-food cases at Wal-Mart. Fifty years later, in "The Physiology of Taste," the French gastronome Jean-Anthelme Brillat-Savarin claimed that cooking made us who we are; by teaching men to use fire, it had "done the most to advance the cause of civilization." More recently, the anthropologist Claude Lévi-Strauss, writing in 1964 in "The Raw and the Cooked," found that many cultures entertained a similar view, regarding cooking as a symbolic way of distinguishing ourselves from the animals.

For Lévi-Strauss, cooking is a metaphor for the human transformation of nature into culture, but in the years since "The Raw and the Cooked," other anthropologists have begun to take quite literally the idea that cooking is the key to our humanity. Earlier this year, Richard Wrangham, a Harvard anthropologist, published a fascinating book called "Catching Fire," in which he argues that it was the discovery of cooking by our early ancestors—not tool-making or language or meat-eating—that made us human. By providing our primate forebears with a more energy-dense and easy-to-digest diet, cooked food altered the course of human evolution, allowing our brains to grow bigger (brains are notorious energy guzzlers) and our guts to shrink. It seems that raw food takes much more time and energy to chew and digest, which is why other primates of our size carry around substantially larger digestive tracts and spend many more of their waking hours chewing: up to six hours a day. (That's nearly as much time as Guy Fieri devotes to the activity.) Also, since cooking detoxifies many foods, it cracked open a treasure trove of nutritious calories unavailable to other animals. Freed from the need to spend our days gathering large quantities of raw food and then chewing (and chewing) it, humans could now devote their time, and their metabolic resources, to other purposes, like creating a culture.

Cooking gave us not just the meal but also the occasion: the practice of eating together at an appointed time and place. This was something new under the sun, for the forager of raw food would likely have fed himself on the go and alone, like the animals. (Or, come to think of it, like the industrial eaters we've become, grazing at gas stations and skipping meals.) But sitting down to common meals, making eye contact, sharing food, all served to civilize us; "around that fire," Wrangham says, "we became tamer."

If cooking is as central to human identity and culture as Wrangham believes, it stands to reason that the decline of cooking in our time would have a profound effect on modern life. At the very least, you would expect that its rapid disappearance from everyday life might leave us feeling nostalgic for the sights and smells and the sociality of the cook-fire. Bobby Flay and Rachael Ray may be pushing precisely that emotional button. Interestingly, the one kind of home cooking that is actually on the rise today (according to Harry Balzer) is outdoor grilling. Chunks of animal flesh seared over an open fire: grilling is cooking at its most fundamental and explicit, the transformation of the raw into the cooked right before our eyes. It makes a certain sense that the grill would be gaining adherents at the very moment when cooking meals and eating them together is fading from the culture. (While men have hardly become equal partners in the kitchen, they are cooking more today than ever before: about 13 percent of all meals, many of them on the grill.)

Yet we don't crank up the barbecue every day; grilling for most people is more ceremony than routine. We seem to be well on our way to turning cooking into a form of weekend recreation, a backyard sport for which we outfit ourselves at Williams-Sonoma, or a televised spectator sport we watch from the couch. Cooking's fate may be to join some of our other weekend exercises in recreational atavism: camping and gardening and hunting and riding on horseback. Something in us apparently likes to be reminded of our distant origins every now and then and to celebrate whatever rough skills for contending with the natural world might survive in us, beneath the thin crust of 21st-century civilization.

To play at farming or foraging for food strikes us as harmless enough, perhaps because the delegating of those activities to other people in real life is something most of us are generally O.K. with. But to relegate the activity of cooking to a form of play, something that happens just on weekends or mostly on television, seems much more consequential. The fact is that not cooking may well be deleterious to our health, and there is reason to believe that the outsourcing of food preparation to corporations and 16-year-olds has already taken a toll on our physical and psychological well-being.

Consider some recent research on the links between cooking and dietary health. A 2003 study by a group of Harvard economists led by David Cutler found that the rise of food preparation outside the home could explain most of the increase in obesity in America. Mass production has driven down the cost of many foods, not only in terms of price but also in the amount of time required to obtain them. The French fry did not become the most popular "vegetable" in America until industry relieved us of the considerable effort needed to prepare French fries ourselves. Similarly, the mass production of cream-filled cakes, fried chicken wings and taquitos, exotically flavored chips or cheesy puffs of refined flour, has transformed all these hard-to-make-at-home foods into the sort of everyday fare you can pick up at the gas station on a whim and for less than a dollar. The fact that we no longer have to plan or even wait to enjoy these items, as we would if we were making them ourselves, makes us that much more likely to indulge impulsively.

Cutler and his colleagues demonstrate that as the "time cost" of food preparation has fallen, calorie consumption has gone up, particularly consumption of the sort of snack and convenience foods that are typically cooked outside the home. They found that when we don't have to cook meals, we eat more of them: as the amount of time Americans spend cooking has dropped by about half, the number of meals Americans eat in a day has climbed; since 1977, we've added approximately half a meal to our daily intake.

Cutler and his colleagues also surveyed cooking patterns across several cultures and found that obesity rates are inversely correlated with the amount of time spent on food preparation. The more time a nation devotes to food preparation at home, the lower its rate of obesity. In fact, the amount of time spent cooking predicts obesity rates more reliably than female participation in the labor force or income. Other research supports the idea that cooking is a better predictor of a healthful diet than social class: a 1992 study in The Journal of the American Dietetic Association found that poor women who routinely cooked were more likely to eat a more healthful diet than well-to-do women who did not.

So cooking matters—a lot. Which when you think about it, should come as no surprise. When we let corporations do the cooking, they're bound to go heavy on sugar, fat, and salt; these are three tastes we're hard-wired to like, which happen to be dirt cheap to add and do a good job masking the shortcomings of processed food. And if you make special-occasion foods cheap and easy enough to eat every day, we will eat them every day.

The time and work involved in cooking, as well as the delay in gratification built into the process, served as an important check on our appetite. Now that check is gone, and we're struggling to deal with the consequences.

The question is, Can we ever put the genie back into the bottle? Once it has been destroyed, can a culture of everyday cooking be rebuilt? One in which men share equally in the work? One in which the cooking shows on television once again teach people how to cook from scratch and, as Julia Child once did, actually empower them to do it?

Let us hope so. Because it's hard to imagine ever reforming the American way of eating or, for that matter, the American food system unless millions of Americans—women and men—are willing to make cooking a part of daily life. The path to a diet of fresher, unprocessed food, not to mention to a revitalized local-food economy, passes straight through the home kitchen.

But if this is a dream you find appealing, you might not want to call Harry Balzer right away to discuss it.

"Not going to happen," he told me. "Why? Because we're basically cheap and lazy. And besides, the skills are already lost. Who is going to teach the next generation to cook? I don't see it.

"We're all looking for someone else to cook for us. The next American cook is going to be the supermarket. Takeout from the supermarket, that's the future. All we need now is the drive-through supermarket."

Crusty as a fresh baguette, Harry Balzer insists on dealing with the world, and human nature, as it really is, or at least as he finds it in the survey data he has spent the past three decades poring over. But for a brief moment, I was able to engage him in the project of imagining a slightly different reality. This took a little doing. Many of his clients—which include many of the big chain restaurants and food manufacturers—profit handsomely from the decline and fall of cooking in America; indeed, their marketing has contributed to it. Yet Balzer himself made it clear that he recognizes all that the decline of everyday cooking has cost us. So I asked him how, in an ideal world, Americans might begin to undo the damage that the modern diet of industrially prepared food has done to our health.

"Easy. You want Americans to eat less? I have the diet for you. It's short, and it's simple. Here's my diet plan: Cook it yourself. That's it. Eat anything you want—just as long as you're willing to cook it yourself."

Michael Pollan, a contributing writer, is the Knight Professor of Journalism at the University of California, Berkeley. His most recent book is "In Defense of Food: An Eater's Manifesto."

THE FARM-RESTAURANT CONNECTION

By Alice Waters

I have always believed that a restaurant can be no better than the ingredients it has to work with. As much as by any other factor, Chez Panisse has been defined by the search for ingredients. That search and what we have found along the way have shaped what we cook and ultimately who we are. The search has made us become part of a community—a community that has grown from markets, gardens, and suppliers and has gradually come to include farmers, ranchers, and fishermen. It has also made us realize that, as a restaurant, we are utterly dependent on the health of the land, the sea, and the planet as a whole, and that this search for good ingredients is pointless without a healthy agriculture and a healthy environment.

We served our first meal at Chez Panisse on August 28, 1971. The menu was pâté en croûte, duck with olives, salad, and fresh fruit, and the meal was cooked by Victoria Wise, who, together with Leslie Land and Paul Aratow, was one of the three original cooks at the restaurant. The ducks came from Chinatown in San Francisco and the other ingredients mostly from two local supermarkets: the Japanese produce concession at U-Save on Grove Street and the Co-op across the street. We sifted through every leaf of romaine, using perhaps 20 percent of each head and discarding the rest. We argued about which olives we ought to use with the duck and settled without much enthusiasm on green ones whose source I don't recall, agreeing after the fact that we could have done better. To this day we have yet to find a source of locally produced olives that really satisfies us.

We don't shop at supermarkets anymore, but in most respects the same processes and problems apply. Leslie Land recalls, "We were home cooks—we didn't know there were specialized restaurant suppliers. We thought everybody bought their food the way we did." I think that ignorance was an important, if unwitting, factor in allowing Chez Panisse to become what it is. Often, we simply couldn't cook what we wanted to cook because we couldn't find the level of quality we needed in the required ingredients, or we couldn't find the ingredients at all. Our set menus, which we've always published in advance so customers

Waters, A. "The Farm-Restaurant Connection," from *Not For Bread Alone*, pp. 96–104. Copyright © 1993 by Ecco Press. Permission to reprint granted by the publisher.

can choose when they want to come, featured the phrase "if available" with regularity during the first seven or eight years. Since we've always felt that freshness and purity were synonymous with quality, there were few guarantees that what we needed would appear in the form and condition we wanted when we wanted it.

If, as I believe, restaurants are communities—each with its own culture—then Chez Panisse began as a hunter-gatherer culture and, to a lesser extent, still is. Not only did we prowl the supermarkets, the stores and stalls of Chinatown, and such specialty shops as Berkeley then possessed (some of which, like the Cheese Board and Monterey Market, predated us and continue to develop from strength to strength) but we also literally foraged. We gathered watercress from streams, picked nasturtiums and fennel from roadsides, and gathered blackberries from the Santa Fe tracks in Berkeley. We also took herbs like oregano and thyme from the gardens of friends. One of these friends, Wendy Ruebman, asked if we'd like sorrel from her garden, setting in motion an informal but regular system of obtaining produce from her and other local gardeners. We also relied on friends with rural connections: Mary Isaak, the mother of one of our cooks, planted fraises des bois for us in Petaluma, and Lindsey Shere, one of my. partners and our head pastry cook to this day, got her father to grow fruit for us near his place in Healdsburg.

Although most of our sources in the restaurant's early days were of necessity unpredictable, produce was the main problem area, and we focused our efforts again and again on resolving it. Perhaps more than any other kind of foodstuff, produce in general and its flavor in particular have suffered under postwar American agriculture. Although we've been able to have as much cosmetically perfect, out-of-season fruit and vegetables as anyone could possibly want, the flavor, freshness, variety, and wholesomeness of produce have been terribly diminished. With the notable exception of Chinese and Japanese markets that even in the early seventies emphasized flavor and quality, we really had nowhere to turn but to sympathetic gardeners who either already grew what we needed or would undertake to grow it for us.

Our emphasis—and, today, our insistence—on organically grown produce developed less out of any ideological commitment than out of the fact that this was the way almost everyone we knew gardened. We have never been interested in being a health or natural foods restaurant; rather, organic and naturally raised ingredients happen to be consistent with both what we want for our kitchen and what we want for our community and our larger environment. Such ingredients have never been an end in themselves, but they are a part of the way of life that inspired the restaurant and that we want the restaurant to inspire. Most of us have become so inured to the dogmas and self-justifications of agribusiness that we forget that, until 1940, most produce was, for all intents and purposes, organic, and, until the advent of the refrigerated boxcar, it was also of necessity fresh, seasonal, and local. There's nothing radical about organic produce: It's a return to traditional values of the most fundamental kind.

It had always seemed to us that the best way to solve our supply problems was either to deal directly with producers or, better still, to raise our own. By 1975, we'd made some progress with the first approach, regularly receiving, for example, fresh and smoked trout from Garrapata in Big Sur. One of my partners, Jerry Budrick, had also set up a connection with the Dal Porto Ranch in Amador County in the foothills of the Sierra Nevada, which provided us with lambs and with zinfandel grapes for the house wine Walter Schug made for us at the Joseph Phelps Winery. Jerry also acquired some land of his own in Amador, and it seemed an obvious solution to our produce needs for us to farm it. In 1977 we tried this, but we knew even less about farming than we thought we did, and the experiment proved a failure.

Fortunately, during the late 1970s some of our urban gardens were producing quite successfully, notably one cultivated by the French gardener and cook at Chez Panisse, Jean-Pierre Moullé, on land in the Berkeley hills owned by Duke McGillis, our house doctor, and his wife, Joyce. In addition, Lindsey Shere returned from a trip to Italy laden with seeds, which her father planted in Healdsburg, thereby introducing us to rocket and other greens still exotic at that time. Meanwhile, we were also learning how to use conventional sources as best we could. Mark Miller, then a cook with us, made the rounds of the Oakland Produce Market each dawn, and we discovered useful sources at other wholesale and commercial markets in San Francisco. Closer to home, we bought regularly—as we still do—from Bill Fujimoto, who had taken over Monterey Market from his parents and had begun to build its reputation for quality and variety.

It's difficult now to remember the kind of attitude to flavor and quality that still prevailed in the mid and late 1970s. When Jeremiah Tower, who was our main cook at Chez Panisse from 1973 to 1977, once sent back some meat he felt wasn't up to scratch, the supplier was apologetic: No one had ever done that before. And Jerry Rosenfield, a friend and physician who has worked on many of our supply problems over the years, caused an uproar one morning when he was substituting for Mark Miller at the Oakland Produce Market: Jerry insisted on *tasting* some strawberries before buying them. Jerry was also a key figure in securing our sources for fish, probably the first of our supply problems that we were able to solve successfully. During the restaurant's first few years, we served very little fish at all, such was the quality available—despite our being across the bay from a city renowned for its seafood. But, in 1975, Jerry brought us some California sea mussels he'd gathered near his home, and they were a revelation. We asked him to bring us more, and in late 1976 he became our fish dealer, buying from wholesalers and fishermen ranging up the coast from Monterey to Fort Bragg. Along the way he began to be assisted by Paul Johnson, a cook from another Berkeley restaurant called In Season, who took over from Jerry in 1979 and who today sells what is arguably the best fish on the West Coast.

Our produce problem, however, remained unsolved, and we decided to have another try at farming. John Hudspeth, a disciple of James Beard who later started Bridge Creek restaurant just up the street from us, owned some land near Sacramento that he was willing to make available to us in 1980 and 1981. In some respects, this farm was a success—producing good onions and potatoes and wonderful little white peaches from a tree John had planted—but we weren't equipped to deal with the valley heat or the land's penchant for flooding. While the farm did produce, it produced unreliably, and we had to continue to obtain supplies from elsewhere. It also finally disabused us of any illusion that we were farmers. We realized that there seemed to be only two solutions available: extending and formalizing the system of urban gardeners we already had in place, and establishing direct connections with sympathetic farmers who could grow what we needed—that is, farmers who, since we didn't know enough farming to do it ourselves, would farm on our behalf.

In the early 1980s, two members of the restaurant staff, Andrea Crawford and Sibella Kraus, and Lindsey Shere's daughter Thérèse established several salad gardens in Berkeley, one of which was in my backyard. These eventually met most of our needs for salad greens, but for other kinds of produce we remained dependent on a hodgepodge of often-unreliable sources. Two things happened in 1982, however, that turned out to be tremendously important. First, Jean-Pierre Gorin, a friend and filmmaker teaching in La Jolla, introduced us to the produce grown near there by the Chino family. And, second, Sibella Kraus became the forager for the restaurant and eventually started the Farm-Restaurant Project. Jean-Pierre happened by the Chinos' roadside stand, tasted a green bean, and arranged to have two boxes sent to us immediately. The beans were exquisite, and I flew down to find out who had grown them. We became good friends, and to this day we receive nine boxes of produce from the Chinos each week.

Meanwhile, as Sibella had become more and more involved with our salad gardens, she decided that she would like to work with produce full-time and proposed that she become the restaurant's first full-time forager, an idea we agreed to with enthusiasm. Sibella spent her time on the road locating farmers, tasting their produce, and, if we liked it, arranging for a schedule of deliveries to Chez Panisse. In 1983, we funded the Farm-Restaurant Project under Sibella's direction, which set up a produce network among a number of Bay Area restaurants and local farmers and culminated in the first Tasting of Summer Produce, now an annual event at which dozens of small, quality-conscious farmers show their produce to the food community and the general public. Sibella left us to work for Greenleaf Produce (from whom we still regularly buy) and has become an important figure in the sustainable-agriculture movement. She was succeeded as forager by Catherine Brandel, who has since become one of the head cooks in our upstairs café. During this period, Green Gulch, run by the San Francisco Zen Center, became an important supplier, as did Warren Weber, whom we continue to work with today. We were also fortunate to have Thérèse Shere and Eric Monrad producing tomatoes, peppers, beans, lettuce, and lamb for us at Coulee Ranch near Healdsburg.

During her tenure as forager, Catherine continued to develop the network Sibella had created, finding, for example, a regular source of eggs for us at New Life Farms. But she was frustrated, as we all were, by the seeming impossibility of finding meat that was both flavorful and raised in a humane and wholesome way. Since the beginning of Chez Panisse, we had been forced to rely on conventional suppliers, a continuing disappointment given how much progress we had made with other kinds of materials. But, in late 1986, Jerry Rosenfield took over as forager from Catherine, and over the next two years he made enormous strides in finding meat sources for us. Jerry had been living in the Pacific Northwest and had discovered a number of ranchers and farmers there who were attempting to raise beef, veal, and lamb without hormones and under humane conditions. In particular, the Willamette Valley between Portland and Eugene, Oregon, became a source for rabbits, lambs, goats, and beef, although Jerry also located producers closer to home, including ones for game and for that most elusive bird—a decently flavored, naturally raised chicken. We still have a way to go, but today, for the first time in our history, we are able to serve meat that really pleases us.

We have made progress on other fronts, too. In 1983, for example, we helped Steve Sullivan launch Acme Bakery, which bakes for us and for many other local restaurants. And, recently, we've realized a close approximation of our dream of having a farm. In 1985, my father, Pat Waters, began looking for a farmer who would be willing to make a long-term agreement to grow most of our produce for us according to our specifications. With help from the University of California at Davis and local organic food organizations, Dad came up with a list of eighteen potential farmers, which he narrowed down to a list of four on the basis of interviews, tastings, and visits. We settled on Bob Cannard, who farms on twenty-five acres in the Sonoma Valley.

Bob is very special, not only because he grows wonderful fruits and vegetables for us— potatoes, onions, salad greens, tomatoes, beans, berries, peaches, apricots, and avocados, to name a few—but also because he is as interested in us as we are in him. He likes to visit the restaurant kitchen and pitch in, and we send our cooks up to him to help pick. He takes all the restaurant's compostable garbage each day, which he then uses to grow more food. He is also a teacher at his local college and a major force in his local farmer's market. He sees that his farm and our restaurant are part of something larger and that, whether we acknowledge it or not, they have a responsibility to the health of the communities in which they exist and of the land on which they depend.

The search for materials continues, and I imagine it always will. We are still looking for good sources for butter, olives, oil, and prosciutto, to name a few. But, even when we find them, the foraging will continue. Ingredients will appear that we'll want to try, and we in turn will have new requirements that we'll want someone to fulfill for us. Whatever happens, we realize that, as restaurateurs, we are now involved in agriculture and its vagaries— the weather, the soil, and the economics of farming and rural communities. Bob Cannard reminds us frequently that farming isn't manufacturing: It is a continuing relationship with nature that has to be complete on both sides to work. People claim to know that plants are living things, but the system of food production, distribution, and consumption we have known in this country for the last forty years has attempted to deny that they are. If our food has lacked flavor—if, in aesthetic terms, it has been dead—that may be because it was treated as dead even while it was being grown. And perhaps we have tolerated such food—and the way its production has affected our society and environment—because our senses, our hearts, and our minds have been in some sense deadened, too.

I've always felt it was part of my job as a cook and restaurateur to try to wake people up to these things, to challenge them really to taste the food and to experience the kind of community that can happen in the kitchen and at the table. Those of us who work with food suffer from an image of being involved in an elite, frivolous pastime that has little relation to anything important or meaningful. But in fact we are in a position to cause people to make important connections between what they are eating and a host of crucial environmental, social, and health issues. Food is at the center of these issues.

This isn't a matter of idealism or altruism but rather one of self-interest and survival. Restaurateurs have a very real stake in the health of the planet, in the source of the foodstuffs we depend on, and in the future of farmers, fishermen, and other producers. Hydroponic vegetables or fish raised in pens will never be a real substitute for the flavor and quality of the ingredients that are in increasing jeopardy today. Professionally and personally, both our livelihoods and our lives depend on the preservation of what we have and the restoration of what we have lost. The fate of farmers—and with them the fate of the earth itself—is not somebody else's problem: It is our fate, too.

There is clearly so much more to do. But ultimately it comes down to realizing the necessity of the land to what we do and our connection to it. Few restaurants are going to be able to create the kind of relationship we have with Bob Cannard, but there are other routes to the same goal. I'm convinced that farmer's markets are an important step in this direction; they also contribute to the local economy, promote more variety and quality in the marketplace, and create community. As restaurateurs and ordinary consumers meet the people who grow their food, they acquire an interest in the future of farms, of rural communities, and of the environment. This interest, when it helps to ensure the continuing provision of open space near cities and the diversity of food produced on it, is to everyone's benefit. Country and city can once again become a mutual support system, a web of interdependent communities. That's why fresh, locally grown, seasonal foodstuffs are more than an attractive fashion or a quaint, romantic notion: They are a fundamental part of a sustainable economy and agriculture—and they taste better, too. Of course, people respond, "That's easy for you to say: In California you can have whatever you want all year round." I tell them that's true, but I also tell them that most of it tastes terrible. And, while there's no reason to forgo all non-locally-produced ingredients—I wouldn't want to give up our weekly shipment from the Chinos—local materials must become the basis of our cooking and our food; this is true for every region of the planet that has produced a flavorful, healthy cuisine.

What sometimes seem to be limitations are often opportunities. Earlier this year, in the lee between the early spring vegetables and those of mid-summer, we had an abundance of fava beans, which we explored in the kitchen for six weeks, served in soups, in purees, as a garnish, and, of course, by themselves—and we discovered that we had only *begun* to tap the possibilities. There was a stew of beans with savory and cream, a fava-bean-and-potato gratin, fava bean pizza with lots of garlic, a pasta fagioli using favas, a rough puree of favas with garlic and sage, and a vinaigrette salad, to name a few. The point is that what constitutes an exciting, exotic ingredient is very much in the eye of the beholder and that few things can be as compelling as fresh, locally grown materials that you know have been raised in a responsible way.

When I was first thinking about opening what would become Chez Panisse, my friend Tom Luddy took me to see a Marcel Pagnol retrospective at the old Surf Theater in San Francisco. We went every night and saw about half the movies Pagnol made during his long career, including *The Baker's Wife* and his Marseilles trilogy—*Marius, Fanny*, and *César*. Every one of these movies about life in the south of France fifty years ago radiated wit, love for people, and respect for the earth. Every movie made me cry.

My partners and I decided to name our new restaurant after the widower Panisse, a compassionate, placid, and slightly ridiculous marine outfitter in the Marseilles trilogy, so as to evoke the sunny good feelings of another world that contained so much that was incomplete or missing in our own—the simple wholesome good food of Provence, the atmosphere of tolerant camaraderie and great lifelong friendships, and a respect both for the old folks and their pleasures and for the young and their passions. Four years later, when our partnership incorporated itself, we immodestly took the name Pagnol et Cie., Inc., to reaffirm our desire to re-create a reality where life and work were inseparable and the daily pace left time for the afternoon anisette or the restorative game of *pétanque*, and where eating together nourished the spirit as well as the body—since the food was raised, harvested, hunted, fished, and gathered by people sustaining and sustained by each other and by the earth itself. In this respect, as in so many others, the producers and farmers we have come to know not only have provided us with good food but have also been essential in helping us to realize our dreams.

PLACE MATTERS

By Amy B. Trubek

I n the act of tasting, when the bite or sip moves through the mouth and into the body, culture and nature become one. Universally, eating (and drinking) is a process of bringing the natural world into the human domain, leading many cultures and religions to focus on the moment of ingestion, for example Kosher dietary rules and Hindu notions of purity and pollution. Unusual to France is the attention put on the role of the natural world in the *taste* of food and drink. When the French take a bite of cheese or a sip of wine, they taste the earth: rock, grass, hillside, valley, plateau. They combine gustatory sensation and the evocative possibilities of taste in their fidelity to the taste of place, or *goût du terroir.*

Place, however, is a poor substitute for *terroir*, a word that merits many definitions in French. *The Concise Oxford Dictionary* defines it as soil, ground, locality, place, or part of the country. The nineteenth-century version of Larousse's *Grand Dictionnaire Universel* defines *terroir* as "the earth considered from the point of view of agriculture." These definitions rely on the natural world, but others focus on the human element. A contemporary French dictionary says *terroir* is either when something has a particular flavor that can be *attributed* to the soil, or the typical tastes and habits that come from a region or a rural area. This approach is longstanding; the nineteenth-century Larousse clarifies the definition of *terroir* with a discussion of *goût du terroir.* This is the "flavor or odor of certain locales that are given to its products, particularly with wine." For example, "Ce vin a un goût du terroir; Je n'y trouve pas le parfum de terroir." [This wine has a local (or site-pecific) taste; I don't smell "place."] Food and drink from a certain place have a unique *flavor.*

These problems of definition do not lie solely with the dictionary compilers. These are difficult words to define because they signify so much to the French. More than words, they are *categories* that frame perceptions and practices—a worldview, or should we say here, a foodview? The agrarian roots of *terroir* best explain the origins and persistence of this foodview. *Terroir and goût du terroir* are categories for framing and explaining people's relationship to the land, be it sensual, practical, or habitual.

France is intensely cultivated. Usable agricultural land still covers the majority of France, 77,803,000 acres in 1985 (Fremont 1996: 3). The nation's geography is described as a combination of urban and rural, and little attention is spent exploring France's "wilderness." The agrarian view dominates. Contemporary French geographer Armand Fremont says: "No other major civilization in Europe or elsewhere has ever valued the soil more than the French or associated it more intimately with the good." Fremont feels that "soil is a focus of all France's thoughts and emotions" (34). A foodview associating taste, soil, and the bounty of the earth thus makes sense.

DESCRIBING *TERROIR* AND CREATING *GOÛT DU TERROIR*

In France, *terroir* is often associated with *racines*, or roots, a person's history with a certain place. This connection is considered essential, as timeless as the earth itself. Agriculturalist Olivier de Serres, in his seventeenth-century treatise, *Le Théâtre d'Agriculture et des Mesnages des Champs* states: "the fundamental task in agriculture is to understand the nature of the *terroir*, whether it is the land of your ancestors or land recently acquired." Soil and roots create the basis of French cuisine as well. Le Grand d'Aussy, in his 1789 work *History of Private Life* discussed French cuisine as the natural fruition of provincial agriculture, tracing back at least two centuries the connection between the cuisine and what "nature has seen fit to allow each of our provinces to produce" (Csergo 1999: 502).

Examining discussions of *terroir* and *goût du terroir* from the eighteenth-century through today, the approach of all the authors, be they journalists, farmers, vintners, chefs, or citizens, is remarkably consistent. Their discourse does not adopt a *point of view*; rather it is considered to *reflect reality*. This fundamentalist view always begins with a defined place, tracing the taste of place back from the mouth to the plants and animals and ultimately back into the soil, creating a very Gallic twist to the oft-used American adage of "location, location, location."

In this discourse, places make unique tastes, and in turn such flavor characteristics and combinations give those places gastronomic renown. *Le Cours Gastronomique*, first published in 1809, includes a map of France that merely outlines the nation's borders and then charts the inner territory solely with agricultural products. Included are the wines of regions such as Bordeaux and the Rhône; Roquefort and Brie are named, with drawings of cheeses, and many charcuterie items are shown as well, such as sausages and cured hams. During the same period, Madame Adanson, in her influential and widely published book *La Cuisinière de la Compagne et de La Ville* lists cheeses by place name: Neufchâtel, Brie, Marolles, Cantal, and specifies the flavor characteristics and methods of proper storage of each. The flavor of the fromage des Vosges, Adanson writes, "is unique among all cheeses; the method of fabrication is a secret of the locality" (1827: 56).

Almost 200 years later, the esteemed *Oxford Companion to Wine* explains terroir as the "much-discussed term for the total natural environment for any viticultural site," where the primary components are soil, topography, and climate (Robinson 1999: 700). Although the Bordeaux, Napa Valley, and South Australia regions all use merlot and cabernet sauvignon grape varietals in their wine, and often similar production methods, their wines taste markedly different. In France, such variations are understood to have everything to do with where the grapevines are planted, hillside or valley, clay or calcareous soil, mild or harsh climate. With *goût du terroir*, location is destiny.

Hugh Johnson, leading wine expert and journalist, embraces this (seemingly) inevitable destiny (as do many other oenophiles). *In A World Atlas of Wine* he explains the varying flavor profiles of French wines with complex descriptions of the geography, climate, and geology: "[Bordeaux's] position near the sea and threaded with rivers gives it a more moderate and stable climate. Forests on the ocean side protect it from strong salt winds and rainfall" (Johnson 2003: 50). Within the region, "the distinctions between different soils and situations produce remarkable difference of flavor and keeping qualities" (Johnson 1983: 45), and finally, at one of the premier chateaus, Chateau Lafite-Rothschild, "Quality starts with the soil: deep gravel dunes over limestone. It [also] depends on the age of the vines: at Lafite an average of forty years" (1983: 60).

For French cheeses, the *goût du terroir* emerges in the type of grasses and wild plants the sheep or goats or cows eat when they are grazing, which depend on the geography of the pasturelands and thus influencing the flavor of the milk. In the pamphlet "Le Gout des Fromages; Le Goût de la France" (The Taste of Cheese; The Taste of France), part of an ongoing series put out by the French Ministry of Agriculture, the very taste of France is said to consist of a "mosaic of regional tastes which derive their flavors from geographical, historical, and cultural roots." The pamphlet goes on to discuss the various products and distinctive dishes of each region in France, providing recipes using local cheeses to show how "the nature of the soil, the climate, and the topography shape the cuisine and flavor." In these analyses, the physical environment (soil, weather, topography), not the tiller of the soil, or the shepherd, or the vintner, are the primary sources in creating the distinctive tastes of French wine and cheese.

CREATING THEIR OWN DESTINY

A closer examination of historical events tells a different story. The natural environment *influences* the flavors of food and beverages, but ultimately the cultural domain, the foodview, creates the *goût du terroir*. The taste of place does not originate with the Mesozoic period collision of the African and European continental plates that defined France's geography and geology. Rather, beginning in the early 1900s, a group of *people* began to organize around this naturalized connection of taste and place, for they saw the potential benefits of a foodview celebrating the agrarian and rural way of life. French *taste-makers*—journalists, cookbook writers, chefs—and *taste producers*—cheese-makers, wine-makers, bakers, cooks—have long been allied in an effort to shape taste perceptions. Taste producers and taste makers intervened in an everyday occurrence, eating and drinking, and these advocates guided the French toward a certain relationship between soil and taste, *le goût du terroir*.

They worked hard to shape French judgments of the morsels and liquids that they put in their mouths. These artisans, critics, and commentators elaborated a new language of taste. This language was never purely aesthetic, however, solely an interaction of taste receptors in the mouth and the brain. These new translations of taste were part of a dialogue with nature. In France, this took place on the edge of their civilized world, the agrarian countryside. They created arguments linking place, taste, types of agriculture and quality that helped protect certain forms of agricultural production, and ultimately, helped to define French national cuisine. These discussions helped shape taste perceptions beyond France as well, for their claims about the taste of place now play an important role in twenty-first-century discussions of food and beverages.

Gastronomic writings of the period expressed these ideas. Madame Pampille says in her charming book, *Les Bons Plats de France: Cuisine Régionale*, first published in 1919, "Il n'est bon gibier que de France" (The only good game is to be found in France), and goes on to assert, "And don't talk to me about the German and Hungarian hares that have infested the markets over the past few years: these are large hares, stupid and without flavor" (1925: 23–24). Found in the "National dishes" chapter, her dictums on quality when it comes to game—that it needs to come from France and be raised in certain environments—disclose an emerging vocabulary and grammar of taste in twentieth-century France. She describes the taste of partridges grown in confined in spaces and fed rapeseed as being faded and dim, whereas the wild (or free) partridges roaming the plains and feeling hunger and thirst, have another taste entirely (1925: 24).

This book is full of recipes certainly, but perhaps it should also be considered a gastronomical treatise, a new physiology of taste in the manner of Brillat-Savarin. Here quality of flavor is linked to location and production style.

And speaking just of the glory and splendor of France and French cuisine is not sufficient for Pampille; distinct geographic regions provide specific taste experiences. The Savoie and Dauphine are lauded for their river trout, whose delicate flesh can only be appreciated when you eat it there. She has even stronger views about bouillabaisse, "the triumph of Marseille, it is only good when eaten in Marseille. Don't try to eat it in Paris" (1925: 143). Place matters.

Rural agricultural practices—a reliance on certain crops or livestock because they responded to the local climate and geography, harvesting the bounty of nearby rivers and seas—became the building blocks of what were named *regional cuisines*. A new connection emerged between agricultural practices, rural life, and food and drink, very much a reaction to the increased urbanization and industrialization of society. This may have been particularly strong in France since agriculture remained a large sector of the economy well into the twentieth-century. Cookbooks, food journalism, and regional food guides were instrumental in developing this regional gastronomy and celebrating the taste of place.

At the turn of the century, Jean Fulbert Dumonteil, journalist and native of the Perigord region wrote: "The Alps and the Pyrenees, the Landes, Cevennes, Auvergne, and the Jura send us small goat cheeses which have a marvelous flavor. The Limousin, Poitou, Bourbonnais, and Berry create sheep cheeses with a fine *saveur*" (1996: 40–41). Using *goût du terroir* to analyze not just individual ingredients or products like cheese and wine, but also dishes, emerges in the same period, a result of a new leisure activity: traveling in the countryside.

Curnonsky was an instrumental figure in the development of regional gastronomy, publishing inventories of regional dishes and guidebooks of stores and restaurants highlighting regional cuisine. The "Prince of Gastronomes," Curnonsky, born Maurice-Edmond Sailland, was the author of numerous books on food and gastronomy in France, publishing in every decade of the twentieth-century until he died in 1956. Included in over fifty works are *La France Gastronomique* (with Marcel Rouff) published in the 1920s, *Le Tresor Gastronomique* (an inventory of regional dishes written with Austin de Croze) in 1933, *Eloge de Brillat-Savarin* in 1931 and *Bon Plats, Bons Vins* in 1950. His life and career spanned a period that witnessed great changes in French cuisine and gastronomy, and he helped make them.

Curnonsky linked the physiology of taste to the particularity of place, taking the everyday practices of locals in various regions of France and creating encyclopedias, guides, and atlases dedicated to advertising and codifying their knowledge. His books are notable for their breadth, with listings of hundreds of recipes, or regional dishes, or restaurants. Depth, on the other hand, is another matter. You never hear the experiences and stories of the people responsible for these recipes, restaurants, or dishes, nor their histories. In his writings the taste of place is made timeless. In *Recettes de Provinces de France* he says, "this work celebrates, in a very artistic fashion, the alliance between tourism and gastronomy I have promoted for fifty years and which is only possible in France, because this is a land of tremendous diversity" (1953: 27).

Curnonsky lived during a period when many in France, from small *chambres de commerce* to corporations, became very interested in the development of rural tourism, linked to the rise in railway and car travel and the growth of urban areas. A gastronomic literature emerges that glorifies the various regions of France during 1910–1930, declaring it part of the glory of the French nation. Some of these efforts were initially part of a larger set of marketing initiatives by Michelin, the tire company, interested in developing various ways of getting people to use their cars to journey into the countryside for purposes of leisure (Harp: 2001). These are the earliest versions of what became the green Michelin guides, references on dining and lodging for all the regions of France, which became powerful arbiters of taste for tourists, French or from abroad. Curnonsky, along with his colleagues Austin de Croze and Marcel Rouff, helped develop regional gastronomy in part to support car and rail travel to the French countryside.

If people were going to leave the cafés and bistros of Paris, Lyon, and Marseille, they needed to have a destination and a celebration in mind—what could be better than wonderful food and wine? Another gastronome of the period, Edmond Richardin, in his book *L'Art du Bien Manger* devotes his introduction to a "gourmet geography of the regions of France." Essentially a prose poem that starts in Flanders and ends in Bearn, Richardin lists the gastronomic wonders of France, region by region: "the andouillettes of Cambrais, the trout of Dunkirk, the triumphant asparagus of Argenteuil." And "onwards to Brittany with its Cancale oysters, lobsters, and langoustines of Roscoff." In Bresse, Bugey, and the land of Gex: "Poulardes de Bresse, Belley sausages, Feillens apples, the cheese of Passin, a rival to the best Gruyère, and the blue cheese of Gex" (1913). He ends by exhorting gourmets to open their minds to the vast gastronomic possibilities of the French provinces.

These ingredients and dishes, now immortalized and codified, came to represent their regions and ultimately guaranteed their permanence, for they came to signify more than a dish using the locally available ingredients (bouillabaisse in and around Marseille, cassoulet in and around Carcasonne), but also to represent the taste of that place, wherever the dish may be consumed. Pampille's admonition to eat bouillabaisse only in Marseille notwithstanding, bouillabaisse became the iconic dish of the French Mediterranean the world over. In the spirit of Proust's madeleine, these ingredients and dishes became iconographic, the *lieux de mémoire* of certain places, their tastes of a France defined as a rich and diverse geography.

Grapes for wine have historically been one of France's largest agricultural products, and apparently *vignerons* were the earliest group of taste producers to realize the possibilities in promoting the link between place and quality; they were the first to take this food-view and use it to their economic advantage. The 1855 Bordeaux wine classifications are generally considered the first attempt by those involved in wine production and sales to promote the quality of wines by their place of origin. These were developed internally by those involved in the Bordeaux wine industry, particularly wine brokers, to be used at the 1855 Exposition Universelle in Paris. These classifications were not monitored by the French state however. The movement to use ideas about place to make arguments about quality became increasingly important in the late nineteenth-century and became part of a serious sociopolitical movement to protect French agricultural products in the early twentieth-century, culminating with the founding of L'Institut National des Appellations d'Origine in the 1930s.

As the link between taste and place evolved in the early twentieth-century, taste producers, particularly the *vignerons*, involved the French state, arguing that legal and political means were needed to protect unique French products from international competition.

They succeeded. The *vignerons* of the Champagne region were the first to use the legal system to create delimitations on production related to locale. The elevated status of champagne amongst the international bourgeoisie in the late nineteenth-century did little to contribute to the livelihoods of the laborers in the fields and much to threaten their identity. Their response was to turn to *terroir*, to fight for champagne as a product of the soil rather than as a placeless pretty label. The *vignerons* wanted to retain some proprietary rights to the name "champagne," now used all over the globe, so they turned to the soil. A series of events, especially the phylloxera epidemic of the 1890s, which threatened *vignerons* and *negotiants* alike, helped legitimize the idea that Champagne as a defined region was fundamental to the identity of champagne as a beverage, nationally or internationally. By 1908 Champagne was granted "the first recognized regional delimitation" (Guy 2003: 150). Certain areas were judged to be in the Champagne region and only wines produced in that area could be sold with the label "Champagne." This came to be the model for protection of wine, cheese, and other products throughout France.

TASTE, *TERROIR*, AND QUALITY

The Institut National des Appellations d'Origine (INAO) has been part of the French Ministry of Agriculture since 1935. Despite the activist legacy behind its creation, the direct result of the organizational efforts of vintners and others, the Institute's philosophy, enumerated in the official literature, is to "protect terroir." As the official literature of 1999 states:

> It has been known from ancient times that certain lands are made more suitable to the creation of products that retain, and in fact, draw out the specific flavors of that place.
>
> Due to this phenomenon, at the beginning of the century, the idea was born to create the notion of appellation d'origine, to acknowledge and protect it under the rubric of *Appellations d'Origines Contrôlées*.

As stated later on, the INAO was created in part to police the link between taste and place: "The INAO was initially charged to *identify* Wines and Eaux de Vie, to *codify* their usage for protection in France and abroad against all encroachments" (emphasis mine). Awarding a wine or cheese or any other food product the status of *Appellation d'Origine Contrôlée* put the official stamp on the connection between taste, locale, and quality.

In an explanation of *Appellations d'Origines Contrôlées* (AOC) and the management of terroir, the INAO states that the AOC system provides the "instruments" growing regions can use to fully take advantage of their resources: "With the extraction of the specifics (or characteristics) of their *terroir*, and the search to value and protect the agricultural possibilities in a geographic zone, AOC products can be genuine instruments for managing and supporting territory." But the consumer also needs to be involved in order for the system to work. Thus, though "standardization leads to delocalization … [and so] supposes that the consumer takes the initiative, recognizes the superiority of a strongly identified product and agrees to pay the price." Therefore, the INAO oversees the local production process but also encourages the consumer to find and appreciate those items. The award of AOC status provides producers in the growing region with the economic, political, technical, and marketing support of a government agency. From the point of view of the INAO, places create distinct tastes. A phenomenon of nature, the mission of the Institute is to be a steward of the relationship between locale and flavor, and to encourage producers and consumers to embrace that concept.

The French foodview linking taste and place possesses a tremendous consistency over the past century, in effect preserving agrarian values and practices now often considered quaint and old-fashioned. Today, the INAO's mission could be seen to preserve a philosophy of production from an earlier era, before the advent of large-scale production, national and international distribution systems, and global consumption patterns. In France, though, the AOC system, and the artisan methods and locale-specific production it champions represent the best of France's agricultural riches. The other possibilities—large-scale industrialized farming, export commodity production of food and wines—is considered anomalous and problematic.

The state plays an important part in the continued possibility of a *goût du terroir* that remains powerful in an era of agriculture characterized by industrialization of practice and globalization of supply. This is a time when McDonald's is not found just on the St.Germain des Près but near Cavaillon in southwest France, and the European Union wants to regulate the size of duck cages used for holding ducks raised for foie gras (or liver) to appease animal rights activists in Britain. French farmers, historically well-organized and culturally powerful, protest regularly against the encroachment of regional and global market forces and regulations on their territory. In a 1999 trade dispute between the US and the EU, the US decided to create a 100 percent tariff for imported European luxury goods, including Roquefort cheese and foie gras. In protest, French farmers attacked a number of McDonald's restaurants in southwest France (the region where foie gras and Roquefort are produced) with rotten apples, tomatoes, and manure. A French farmer was quoted in the *New York Times* as saying: "My struggle remains the same … the battle against globalization and for the right of people to feed themselves as they choose" (Cohen 1999).

How do the French keep fidelity to the *goût du terroir* in the face of all these changes? There are many strategies, and most revolve around the persistent commitment to traditional production methods, thus preserving what is now considered the *historical* quality of local flavors. Thus, there exists but one way to make a true cassoulet or bouillabaisse, only one place to find the real Roquefort cheese, only one type of red wine that truly speaks of

"Bordeaux." Authenticity dominates the discourse when French food and wine producers talk about their wines, cheeses, foie gras, and more. In this case, authenticity is primarily determined by the production locale, though the "authentic identity" of the person making the cheese or wine comes under discussion as well.

LOOKING FOR HOME

If you look at the link between taste and place made today, this association clearly contains a dimension of nostalgia. And such nostalgia extends beyond a taste memory for certain foods and drinks of a region, but also for a certain way of life. Barbara Kirschenblatt-Gimblett's definition of "heritage" can help make sense of why *goût du terroir* continues to be embraced in France: "Heritage is a 'value added industry'; heritage produces the local for export; heritage is a new mode of cultural production in the present that has recourse to the past" (1998: 149–53). The foodview based on *terroir and goût du terroir* initially elaborated a century ago as a means of protecting, preserving, and promoting artisan practices and regional identities allows the French, now primarily living in cities and towns, to flirt with a lifestyle more representative of the past than the present.

Local taste, or *goût du terroir*, is now evoked when an individual wants to remember an experience, explain a memory, or express a sense of identity. People themselves can possess the taste of their birthplace, or *"sentir le terroir."* Despite their often very modern; urban lifestyles, the French retain a powerful connection to the land of their ancestors. *Gourmet* magazine explains to its American audience: "Even the most urbane boulevardier can become near maudlin about his *terroir*, acknowledging roots reaching back to a province, a village, a family vegetable patch … his allegiance to the land of his fathers remains intact." In this form, "taste" in France mediates between the body and culture: the gustatory moment incorporates people's belief that the very soil, plants, climactic conditions, and animals make France a unique piece of the Earth, rather than a nation among many others. And for the French, the moment when the Earth travels to the mouth is a time of reckoning with their local memory and identity.

In an interview with the operators of a small press that prints books related to the Dordogne region, including cookbooks, they argued that the emphasis on *"terroir* has increased in the past thirty years, and it is primarily a form of nostalgia; people are searching for their *racines* or roots as an anecdote to their increasingly fast-paced, urban lives." Only in the last ten years, they argued, have urban sophisticates begun to embrace *cuisine du terroir*. Earlier it was considered uncomplicated peasant food, heavy and often bland and not of interest for cosmopolitan French people. The twenty-first-century understanding of the taste of place adopts the long-held view that places within France create unique flavors, only now celebrating these flavors increasingly involves rejecting the trappings of modernity and returning to earlier ways.[1]

In France, taste thus is a form of local knowledge. The success of the taste producers lies in their ability to create an association between place and quality. They appropriated the link between taste and place, and helped create legal and governmental mechanisms to champion location-based food and beverages. Thus today, local tastes define superior quality, which means the French are willing to pay a higher price. Burgundy wines are known to have different taste profiles than wines from Bordeaux and Languedoc, though all may be red wines. In contrast, Americans do not associate specific locales with flavor profiles in wine, rather they buy and taste according to grape varietal: Pinot Noir, Merlot, etc. The French also perceive that goods produced locally using a smaller scale of production are superior. An AOC wine produced from a single vineyard in Bordeaux is considered better than a blended wine from vineyards all over the Languedoc. Wine producers and consumers use *terroir* as an ordering and evaluative concept when it comes to quality of flavor, to the point that now in France *terroir* is used as a major means of marketing wines and asserting their quality. The main marketing slogan for the AOC region Coûteaux du Languedoc, located outside of Montpellier, is "L'art de faire parler le terroir" (The art of expressing the soil). Local taste is worth the price.

GOÛT DU TERROIR: NATURE OR CULTURE?

People's investments—cultural and economic—made the French word for soil signify so much: a sensibility, a mode of discernment, a philosophy of practice and an analytic category. *Terroir* and *goût du terroir* represent the gastronomic glory of France. What they *say* may embrace the timeless and essential notion of mother Earth, but what they have *done* is create a vision of agrarian rural France and convincingly put it in people's mouths.

The more I think about taste and place, however, the more I wonder if *goût du terroir* transcends France. The historical particulars of the "production of locality" are certainly unique to France, along with the tremendous cultural commitment to the notion. But when it comes to the idea that quality of flavor is linked to locally based, small-scale production that pays attention to natural conditions, I wonder if the French have captured and bottled, so to speak, a powerful dimension of taste more broadly defined. Along those lines, I would like to tell a story. Several years ago I was asked to speak to a group of professionals who run the food service at a leading Ivy League university. I discussed the importance of thinking about food from a cultural and historical perspective. As an introduction to the next event, a port tasting led by the school's sommelier, I spoke briefly about my research on *goût du terroir* in France and the AOC system. The director of the university food service, savvy to the importance of marketing in America to create elite market niches for certain products, looked at me skeptically, and said, "They are just trying to sell the sizzle and not the steak."

I stayed for the tasting and sat next to the director. The sommelier led us through a tasting of four different ports. (Though produced in Portugal, ports are subject to a control system similar to the French *Appellations d'Origine Contrôlées,* in fact some consider the system for port to be the historical precursor of that in France.) He began with two fairly inexpensive blended ports produced in large quantities. The third port was a vintage port, which means it was created from an unusually good harvest. Every year could be labeled "vintage"; however not every year is declared a vintage year because conditions were not considered favorable for producing high-quality wines. All the grapes came from a single vineyard (most ports are made from grapes picked in a number of vineyards), and only 39,000 bottles were produced, a very small quantity. The sommelier gave us this information, and we tasted the port.[2] After tasting two blended non-vintage ports, you could truly taste a difference. There was greater clarity and depth to the flavor. The Director looked at me, laughed, and said, "OK it's not just the sizzle. This port simply tastes better." Thousands of miles away, part of a culture with a very different foodview, we tasted place and understood quality.[3]

NOTES

1. It could be argued that *goût du terroir* has come to define an aspect of French identity that is locally defined, but is ultimately part of the national project to preserve and promote "Frenchness" in all its forms. In Arjun Appadurai's terms, the "production of locality" through taste helps constitute the meaning of "France."
2. It was a 1990 Quinta do Vesuvio Vintage Porto, stamped bottle number 14, 295.
3. Thanks to Priscilla Parkhurst Ferguson and Kyri Claflin for their thoughtful readings of an earlier draft of this chapter.

REFERENCES

Adanson, Aglae (L. E. Audot) (1827), *La Cuisinière de la Campagne et de la Ville,* Paris: Audot.

Appadurai, Arjun (1996), *Modernity at Large,* Minneapolis: University of Minnesota Press.

Cadet de Gassicon, Charles-Louis (1808), *Cours Gastronomique, ou les Diners de Manant-Ville,* Paris: Capelle et Renand.

Csergo, Julia (1999), "The regionalization of cuisines," in *Food: A Culinary History,* (ed.) J. L. Flandrin and M. Montanari, New York: Columbia University Press 502.

Cohen, Roger (1999), "Fearful over the future, Europe seized on food," *New York Times,* August 29, (4), 1.

Curnonsky (1950), *Bon Plats, Bon Vins,* Paris: M. Ponsot.

Curnonsky and Rouff, Marcel (1921), *La France Gastronomique,* Paris: F. Rouff.

Curnonsky and de Croze, Austin (1933), *Le Trésor Gastronomique.* Paris: Librairie Delagrave.

Curnonsky (1953), *Recettes de Provinces de France,* Paris: Les Productions de Paris.

Dumonteil, Jean Fulbert (1996), *Le Perigord Gourmand,* Castelnaud: L'Hydre.

Ferguson, Priscilla Parkhurst (1998), "A cultural field in the making: gastronomy in nineteenth-century France," *American Journal of Sociology*, 104: 3 (November).

Fremont, Armand (1996–98), "The land," *Realms of Memory: Rethinking the French Past*, (ed.) by Pierre Nora, New York: Columbia University Press, 2–36.

Guy, Kolleen (2003), *When Champagne Became French*, Baltimore: Johns Hopkins University Press.

Harp, Stephen (2001), *Marketing Michelin: Advertising and Cultural Identity in France*, Baltimore: Johns Hopkins University Press.

Institut National des Appellations d'Origine (1999), Official literature.

Johnson, Hugh (1983), *Modern Encyclopedia of Wine*, New York, Simon and Schuster.

___. (2003), World Atlas of Wine, London: Mitchell Beazley.

Kirschenblatt-Gimblett, Barbara (1998), *Destination Culture: Tourism, Museums, Heritage*, Berkeley: University of California Press.

Le Cours Gastronomique ou Les Divers de Menant-Ville (1809), Paris: Capelle et Renand.

Pampille, Mme. (1925), *Les Bons Plats de France: Cuisine Régionale*, Paris: Fayard.

Richardin, Edmond (1913), *La Cuisine Française du XlVe au XXe Siècle*, Paris: Editions de l'Art et Littérature.

Robinson, Jancis (ed.) (1999), *The Oxford Companion to Wine*, Oxford: Oxford University Press.

Serra, Sylvie (2000), Interview, Dordogne, March.

Serres, Olivier de (1600/1805), *Le Théâtre d'Agriculture et des Mesnages des Champs*, Paris: Societé d'Agriculture de la Seine.

TASTE IN AN AGE OF CONVENIENCE

From Frozen Food to Meals in 'the Matrix'

By Roger Haden

The use, understanding, and experience of the sense of taste has been and continues to be shaped within particular historical contexts by means of specific technologies: technoscientific and discursive, artefactual, and conceptual. To situate taste in the contemporary Western context therefore requires consideration of the major forces (contingent upon such technologies) which on a number of levels have affected the experience of taste. Firstly, both modern and postmodern food cultures need to be conceived of in relation to radical changes to food production techniques and to modes of consumption. Secondly and due in part to the modern separation of food producers from food consumers, the ways in which meanings ascribed to foods have been constructed via the mediation of advertising, packaging, and food-related discourses need to be assessed. These have contributed significantly to altering Western attitudes and responses to the experience and understanding of taste. It has often been stated that once nutritional needs are met, the capacity of food to take on a plethora of culturally specific meanings pushes it beyond its role as nutrient and into that of being a 'language'. In the pursuit of profit and through various media, commercial enterprise has exploited the fact that food is a mode of communication, one which continues to drive the sale of new food products. The sense of taste has been configured within such a context.

THE TASTE OF CONVENIENCE

The main marketing plank of the twentieth-century marriage between the production of food and the consumption of food-related images was 'convenience', a hugely flexible term which could not merely be applied to foods, but to all goods and services supposed to 'make life easier'. Technologies, products and even flavours and images could embody or at least express a notional convenience. Sweet foods like soft drinks were construed as providing 'easy energy', along with being fun, for example.[1] More generally, so-called convenience foods became synonymous with saving effort, time, and money and with ending the 'drudgery' of home cookery.

By the 1920s, American families were consuming significant quantities of tinned and frozen convenience foods, although the production techniques used proved to be of cost-saving convenience primarily to industry, rather than to consumers. Freezing could halt the deterioration of foods already 'going off', for example. Additionally, crude food processing succeeded in leaching out taste, colour, and nutrients. Public awareness of such deficiencies hampered any hoped-for boom in sales. Therefore, stopping frozen foods from 'deteriorating into an ugly mess when the food thawed' would become a crucial public image issue for industry (Levenstein 1993: 106–107).

By 1929, Massachusetts-based inventor Clarence Birdseye 'had developed his plate freezer. The modern phase of food freezing with retail packaging and quick and deep cooling down to minus 18 °C (0 °F) begins from this date' (Borgstrom 1969: 41). Snap-freezing and colourfast printing helped greatly to redeem the image of frozen foods. Birdseye developed a moistureproof cellophane wrapping which allowed foods to be frozen more quickly, while the waxed cardboard used for the outer packaging prevented thawing products from becoming misshapen. Birdseye chose to call his products 'frosted' rather than using the pejorative term 'frozen' and also designed display freezer cabinets that would be mass-produced for supermarkets. Filled with a range of meat, fish, fruit, and vegetable products, supermarket freezers 'became the "miracle" that produced fresh foods out of season and changed eating habits so radically …' (Shephard 2000: 303).

During World War II, industrial freezing, dehydrating, and canning were scaled to help provide food for the military, while the upward trend in postwar frozen food sales were in part the result of adopting such technologies to service a growing civilian populace. In terms of consumption, frozen convenience foods triumphed, facilitated by the use of the car and the spread of supermarkets and further encouraged by television advertising and by the return of individual earning power: 'By 1959 Americans were buying $2.7 billion worth of frozen foods a year … 2700 per cent more than in 1949' (Levenstein 1993: 108). A growing number of ready-to-heat meals were showcased, 'retouched' products that could attract shoppers with colourful promises and photographic images of foods: information they could 'consume' prior to actual consumption. Such products lined the supermarket aisles making possible the 'grazing' phenomenon of the 1970s. During the same decade the microwave oven (an unforeseen by-product of 1940s radar science) added a functional, networked link within a technological matrix of food processing, information, convenience, and consumption. 'Freezer-to-table' microwave foods, in particular, would become a multi-billion dollar industry in the 1980s.

Today, still underpinning the empire of food-processing industries is the technological means to drive marketing and to make things look and taste to industry specifications. Indeed, 'convenience food' now depends on a specialized flavour industry:

About 90 per cent of the money that Americans spend on food is used to buy processed food … since the end of World War II, a vast industry has arisen in the United States to make processed food palatable. Without this flavour industry, the fast-food industry could not exist.

(Schlosser 2001: 121)

This industry was engendered in the 1960s with the development of new technologies for commercial use (principally, mass spectroscopy and gas chromatography) which eventually enabled scientists to create thousands of artificially produced colourings and flavourings. So-called 'natural food flavours' could thereby be chemically copied. While product labels which boasted 'natural flavour' might have reassured consumers, this information could also be misleading, since the chemical reproduction of natural flavours capitalized on a loophole in labelling laws. With chemical solvents used to isolate a natural food's flavour compounds, that flavour could then be replicated. Sold under the appellation of 'natural flavour', any number of artificial tastes could, technically speaking, be added to any food (the latter being treated as merely a substrate). Furthermore, a base-product like milk could be flavoured, texturized, cooked, whipped, aerated or frozen, while other food items, like soy beans, could be used to create various 'milk' products—a process industry would call *interconversion* (Cantor and Cantor 1967: 445). Loath to rely on the inconsistency and quality variability of seasonal produce as a source of revenue and keen to extend the perishable life of food, industry has opted for the technoscience of preservation, product manipulation through the use of various forms of processing, artificial additives, and chemical agents. As a result, the taste of a particular food product can bear little relationship to that of a 'real' (that is, unprocessed) product.

Of course, there is no question as to whether the industrialization and historical advance of the sciences involved in food production, processing, preservation, storage, and transportation represent a positive advance. Indeed, a modern revolution of the food system underpins our present-day food habits and diet. Absolute availability, continuity, food quality, and price have (at least in theory) seemingly banished the problem of absolute need, of nutritionally poor food and of the general scarcity of food commonplace in the premodern West.[2] Notwithstanding, the provision of better foods is in fact no guarantee of better health or well-being. Commerce and industry do not always act in the interests of health. Excessive 'consumption' has brought many diet-related ills.

In this context, legislation related to label misrepresentation, for example, always seems to lag behind the aggressive and 'strategic' connotative marketing adopted to continuously make products attractive to consumers. Today, a product's 'no-fat' guarantee may be disguising the nutritional deficiency of a food which is packed full of many unhealthy additives, including sugar. Moreover, a consumer's reception of product images is typically that related to a large range of similarly processed foods, like bread, with each bread 'type' being packaged merely to look different. Following Marx, we could say that commodity-appeal (and desire for convenience) overtakes our experience of the tangible qualities of smell and taste and touch. 'In the desert of modern life things take the place of affections and feelings and quantity has to compensate for quality', writes Piero Camporesi (Camporesi 1998: 186). In his bleak assessment of contemporary supermarket shopping, it is the 'superficial and distracted' senses of hearing and sight which have 'abolished touch' and 'eliminated smell …the most delicate senses' (171).

IF SEEING IS BELIEVING, WHERE DOES THAT LEAVE TASTE?

Taste relations—that is, the sum of those factors affecting the experience of taste within the mediating world (or context) in which it operates—have entered a brave new world. At the same time, this can sometimes imply the reinscription of even centuries-old prejudices, like the ennobling of the ocular and auditory senses above the 'animal' senses of taste and smell, for example. As if reconfirming this historically philosophic understanding, Australia-based biscuit manufacturer Arnott's now advertises its cocktail crackers, 'Shapes', with the byline: 'Flavour you can see'. Starkly attesting to an ability to commodify food and flavour as 'image', such marketing reinforces cultural perceptions of what characterizes a particular sense modality (in this case, both taste and sight); what it can experience and how this occurs; and the nature of what that sense might contribute to knowledge. Exposure to the coded signs of advertising can thereby also serve to determine the experience of each of the sense modalities themselves. In this instance, sensory interdetermination is marked by a kind of gustatory 'mimesis', whereby taste's knowledge of its putative objects is eclipsed.

Additionally, a recent trend in advertising has been to give expression to the notion of 'no-frills' hedonism and guilt-free pleasure. By representing particular sensory *affects* which connote a kind of maximization of intense feelings, sensations and pleasures, one advertisement for Pioneer hi-fi, for example, celebrates such corporeal pleasures by configuring taste. It depicts, in close-up, parted red lips, before which slender feminine fingers poise a single red—presumably 'hot'—chilli pepper. The ad claims that 'Pioneer makes them hotter than this' and conflates sound, taste and sexual allure with a supposedly hip sense of the contemporary music scene. The ad promises a gamut of 'sensory' pleasures: 'Hotter Chilli Peppers. Juicier Cranberries. And the smashingest Pumpkins'.

The possibilities for multiplying both the material qualities and semio-logical connotations of edible objects are today virtually limitless and so bring about profound changes to diet, often by interrelated means. Conjured up in the space between the product-sign and consumer consciousness, 'tastes' themselves—like sweetness, creaminess or the 'crisp'—act as representations: predigested in the sense that they are already the products of conditioned consumer responses; popular tastes which act as 'interpreters' in the consumer's experience of taste (Barthes 1979: 69–70). Our cultural common sense of what gustation is and of what it can know, changes accordingly. Subject to the literal and semiotic manipulation of food as sign and as thing, various new and altered 'tastes' emerge, influenced by the mix 'n' match production logic of industry.

Displacing any reasoned sensory engagement with food are the food-related discourses we willingly—but often unreflectively—enter into at the surface of things. In terms of taste, advertising mantras promise that products will deliver on pleasure, sensation, and satisfaction, yet semiotically, they also trade on fears, phobias, and anxieties linked to such issues as weight, health, beauty, and social status. The ultimate cost of this mediation by advertising—between us, our food, and our sense of taste—is that the total complement of possible gustatory experiences (which both nature and culinary craft provide) is circumscribed by contrived and prescriptive standards of taste set by media constructions of 'health', and 'beauty'. Routinely associated with food and eating, such ideals can cause the individual anxiety and even illness.[3] Whether we earnestly regulate our eating habits according to available dietary advice or are duped into an excessive food consumption pattern by the unrelenting commercialized command to 'Eat, enjoy!' or even knowingly indulge our appetite for food in an 'ignorance is bliss' fashion, the mediation of taste by applied technoscience, slogans, images, and advice in effect trivializes taste as both flavour and as sensory faculty.

Typically, taste appears to have been recast as simply a sensory *effect*: that is, as a sensation cut off from the wider ambit of taste's functions as a mode of knowing. In both Ayurvedic medicine and traditional Chinese medicine, tastes themselves are understood to have specific medicinal values. The trivialization of taste in the West not only sets this knowledge of taste adrift from pharmacology, but inscribes the notion that in the everyday understanding and experience of an individual's sense of taste, 'sensation' is the raison *d'être of gustation*. KFC's 'Zinger' chicken-burger, for example, is described as 'the taste bud thumper', while its deep-fried 'popcorn chicken' is advertised as being 'mouth-poppin' fun for ya tongue'. Such a trivialization also points to the potentially dangerous affiliation of drug, food, sign and sensory effect, a 'cocktail' that already serves as the model for many so-called smart foods and drinks.

In a wider historical context, the culinary-cultural legacy of the knowledge gained through the sense of taste has been one related to all those practices, technologies, and experiences that have affected taste; taken together, this represents our present-day 'archive of taste'.[4] The *'commodification of sensation'* is a phrase suggestive of how the fragile, 'chemical' history of taste is being usurped by simulations, as the focus is tightened on the immediacy of thrilling sensations. Chemical additives simulate the qualities of tastes, textures, and other gustatory sensations, as the experience of tasting an actual food, of thinking about that food and of the way it tastes, becomes an impossibility.[5] Ultimately, such contrivance not only detracts from the appreciable diverse pleasures and healthful benefits gained through savouring flavours and foods; it also subtracts from the very possibility of knowing-through-taste. The senses require an 'aesthetic education'—as some European countries offer—rather than the shock tactics of industry. *Homo sapiens*, the *knowing* human, is simultaneously the tasting human; and we should think before we taste. However, the powers at work in the world of taste today encourage an everyday forgetting of the senses, which is now the behavioural norm.

As taken-for-granted 'media', the senses have themselves become *mediatized*. What we therefore now meet halfway, as it were, is a product's image, a powerfully motivating force in choice-making. As if by default, in relation to taste, we opt for the visual aesthetics of the big, bright, and blemish-free. However, this overemphasis on the visual signs of quality has also misled consumers. The efforts of producers to make even natural foods like fruits and vegetables appear 'perfect', has in recent decades contributed to, as it has (perhaps ironically) obscured the fact that a marked decline in the nutritional value of these products has also been discovered. Having studied scientific records of plant analysis dating back to 1940, British researcher David Thomas discovered 'stunning declines' of trace elements in 'all fruits and vegetables'. Supposedly one of the vegetable kingdom's most nutritious members, broccoli, had lost seventy-five per cent of its calcium in the intervening years, for example (Engel 2001). Copper, sodium, and magnesium were also shown to be in decline in many other vegetables and fruits. Modern agribusiness, artificial fertilizers and hydroponics are obviously geared for speedy growing and breeding (for looks, size, and colour) while such processes adversely affect nutritional content. More importantly with regard to flavour, the taste complexity produced by natural processes of idiosyncratic growth and maturation, soil and climate is lost, constantly losing ground—or perhaps one might say *terroir*—to 'looks'. Our palates and tongues are 'dumbing down', no longer able to judge or enjoy the living vitality and potential flavour variance of foods produced outside the networks of the industrial-commercial matrix. Combined in so many processed foods, the obliterating power of sugar, salt, and fat (a seemingly perennial taste triumvirate) are complemented by cheap 'filler' and artificial flavour. Such foods seem designed to replace gustatory sensitivity with a taste bud 'thumping'. With recourse to high-speed data-processing of consumer-sourced information and to lab statistics based on tests using bionic 'noses' and 'tongues', food product research, development, design and marketing strategies rapidly advance. Well synchronized, the invention, processing, packaging, transportation, and retailing of food products takes place within a seamless web of operations which also *produces* taste.

If it is to be valued as a corporeal sense, we must be careful not to reduce taste in this way. Sensory effects and personal tastes, do not sufficiently account for taste as a mode of knowing. We must not trivialize, but seek to acknowledge the material history involved here. Taste is as much a product of taste-related cultural and technological forces as it is of ideas like 'convenience'; of philosophical prejudices (like that which ennobles sight, but not gustation); and of the related forms of *separation* (social, economic, and political) which appear to be fundamental to capitalist economics. It is within this wider context that the potential uses and pleasures of sensory taste must be situated; indeed, recognized and explored.

Unfortunately and with regard to taste, the information age has compounded separations; perhaps most fundamentally, that between sign and substance. A new 'state' pervades, which both Jean Baudrillard and Umberto Eco have designated as 'hyperreality'. Baudrillard writes:

> The world of the pseudo-event, of pseudo-history and of pseudo-culture ... a world ... produced not from the fluctuating and contradictory nature of reality, but *produced as artefacts from the technical manipulation of the medium and its coded elements*. It is this and nothing else, which defines all signification whatsoever as *consumable*.
>
> (Baudrillard 1990: 92)

The media, but also Western culture (viewed as a communication system) functions according to this logic, whereby the multiplication and over-determination of signs, as much as their 'consumption', is simply a necessity. Media reality demands this 'nourishment', which typically takes the form of advertising and whereby the blurring of fact and fiction becomes absolute. Daniel Boorstin once described advertising as 'the characteristic rhetoric of democracy' (cited in Borgmann 1984: 53). The incessant production of thousands of 'new and exciting' food products and ideas (and of convenience meals in the guise of 'old favourites') also makes good the sociologist Niklas Luhmann's statement that '[A]fter truth comes advertising' (Luhmann 2000: 44). In effect, consumer understanding and appetites are continually exposed to recursive forms of mediation which undermine any real freedom (of choice); the momentary elation felt as an effect of attaining the 'free', the 'best value' or of experiencing a 'taste sensation', suggests an even greater need for the repetition of such feelings.

This promise of 'elation' has also often been linked to technology and, as a supposed by-product of the latter, to 'convenience'. When, in the 1970s, the 'futuristic' microwave oven became a popular icon of modern convenience (and a commercial success some twenty years after its invention), selling it required a heavy reliance on images of conventionally cooked foods (roasted or grilled, for example). This 'magic' was required because 'the microwave' could not actually cook like its electric or gas counterparts. It left foods flaccid and looking 'uncooked'. Even though 'the nuker' would in practice be used less for actual cookery than for the reheating of pre-packaged and processed convenience foods, it was hailed as 'the greatest cooking discovery since fire' (no author cited 1975: 9). In the US, 'microwaves' would outsell conventional ovens in 1975, thus turning a 'culinary' fiction into a social fact. The only 'cookery' worth noting here is that which combines advertising and industrial technoscience in an attempt to win over consumers.

In the 1950s, Roland Barthes coined the word 'myth' to describe the modern overdetermination of 'things' by 'signs'. 'Myth is a *value*', Barthes wrote 'and truth is no guarantee for it; nothing prevents it from being a perpetual alibi' (Barthes 1972: 123). Barthes conceived the alibi as a representational form of truth which, signified by the product, lent the latter an appealing honesty by connoting some historical or cultural 'truth' or a functional attribute. Industrially produced pasta, for example, might carry with it a logo-alibi suggesting simple, peasant food. Barthes refers to the alibi as a 'constantly moving turnstile', in that nothing in the nature of myth stops the alibi's turning or figuratively speaking, troping (Barthes 1972: 123). 'Good home cooking' can thereby easily be 'turned' into parody. But perhaps this only infers that the experience of food and taste is always interpreted through images and texts; whereby, as fundamental aspects of the *psychological mediation* of eating, imagination builds or weakens appetite. Food may not have to be good to think before it is eaten, but arguably it must on some level be thought. However, in the age of convenience cookbooks would make a mockery of 'origins', exploiting representations of the exotic for commercial ends. After the Second World War, recipes designated *à la française*, for example, could use 'garlic' as an alibi. While only a hint of this culinary bulb might be specified in the recipe, the presence of the status-term 'garlic' was enough to connote French sophistication. 'Mexican chicken' with pineapple, avocado, bananas, grapes, chilli powder, and cinnamon and Tahitian chicken with rum and currants were typical examples of a cruder form of semiotic seasoning (Mason 1955).

Commenting on the recipe form, Luce Giard explains that this kind of allocation of culinary-gustatory values 'is not strictly analytic and explanatory'. More importantly, '… it designates someplace other than here'; a kind of culinary *fort da*, establishing the play of desire within a symbolic geography of food (de Certeau et al. 1998: 222). Indeed, as Barthes noted in his discussion of myth, 'there never is any contradiction, conflict, or split between the meaning and the form: they are never at the same place' (Barthes 1972: 123). 'Tahitian chicken' is the imaginary scene where meaning inscribes the form of food. Like the recursiveness of the media, this use of language equally implies how particular *tastes* can act metaphorically. Serving as advertising referents, *tastes* appear to have a sustaining semiotic power, while the substance of food itself can ebb away, as it were, into *taste-signs*. In the late 70s, microwave cookbook author, Ginger Scribner, took pains to endorse the purchase and use of specialist convenience foods like 'liquid smoke', 'instant tea', and 'dehydrated salad mix'. (Scribner 1978: 6–7).

More recently, of the 11,000 new food products introduced into the market in the US in 1998, over 'two-thirds were condiments, candy and snacks, baked goods, soft drinks, and dairy products (cheese products and ice cream novelties)' (Nestlé 2002: 25). Even though some of these products are sold on the premise of being 'low-fat' or 'no-salt' or are claimed to be nutritionally enhanced with vitamins ('enhancement' now suggests so-called functional foods and nutroceuticals as well), Marion Nestlé argues it is the promotion of sales which drives the need to create such products. Both image and the delivery of gustatory thrills, combined, have become the 'new taste'. The detrimental outcomes of such a marriage are clearly evident: diet-related illnesses among children have climbed rapidly in recent years. While at least since the dawn of industrialization, the commercial imperative has spurred on those willing to adulterate foods for profit, in the era of bioengineering such products fall under a new appellation: 'franken-foods'. According to bioengineering gurus, genetic 'recipes' will make entirely new foods possible: 'Kid-friendly foods are on the way. Researchers will develop tastier vegetables, such as chocolate carrots and pizza-flavoured corn' (Toops 1998: 71).

MEALS IN 'THE MATRIX'

For the purposes of enlightenment and entertainment, science fiction filmmakers have milked the ideological implications of so-called franken-food, which (at least in the science-fiction genre) has often been equated with a single food, 'scientifically designed' to answer all dietary needs. Ever since French chemist, Marcellin Berthelot (1827–1907), looked forward to the day when modern chemistry would reduce the human diet to a little white pill', products like the green pap which constituted the diet in the film *Soylent Green* (dir. Richard Fleischer 1973) have been depicted in order to satirize such utopian bravado (Berthelot 1894). The pap in this case turns out to be made from processed human bodies. This type of story no doubt highlights the fear that if some 'superfood' were produced which could sustain us all, the 'law' of social inequality suggests that any such 'us all' (once called 'the masses') would soon be established as a readily exploitable majority. Yet, even the glamorous technological décor of Stanley Kubrick's *2001: A Space Odyssey* (1968) is belied by the sombre sucking of crewmen who eat through straws or scrape coloured pap from colourfully labelled dispenser trays. Closer to home, so to speak, liquefied spacefood with appetizing names like 'Chicken Salad Spread' now narrows the technological gap between the fantasy and reality of such 'superfoods' (see: http://spacelink.nasa.gov—accessed 20.10.00).

One recent film in the tradition mentioned, *The Matrix* (dirs. Andy and Larry Wachowski 1999) parodies current technologies, conventions and beliefs related to food, fantasy, and reality. The so-called matrix is a 'neural interactive simulation' which has been imposed on Earth by 'the machines'. The matrix allows 'humans' to think themselves to be real, living as they do, vicariously, immersed in an artificial world. If one chooses, this includes eating a beautifully cooked steak and drinking good red wine in a classy restaurant. However, in reality, the machines are using the ecologically devastated Earth as the base for growing actual human babies in a 'battery': a vast womb-like incubator which in turn produces the vital homiothermic energy needed by the machines to power the matrix with electricity.

While planning to overcome the machines, a small band of would-be heroes eke out a precarious existence in a spacecraft, evading 'sentinels' in a netherworld outside the matrix.

At breakfast, the crew dish themselves a mucous-like substance, pumped from a dispenser and described as 'everything the body needs':

TANK: Here you go buddy. Breakfast of champions. If you close your eyes it almost feels like you're eating runny eggs.

APOC: (interrupts) Yeah or a bowl of snot.

MOUSE: You know what it really reminds me of? Tasty Wheat. Did you ever eat Tasty Wheat?

SWITCH: No, but technically neither did you.

MOUSE: That's exactly my point, exactly! Because you have to wonder now, how did the machines really know what Tasty Wheat tasted like? Maybe they got it wrong. Maybe what I think Tasty Wheat tasted like actually tasted like oatmeal or, ah, tuna fish. That makes you wonder about a lot of things. You take chicken, for example. Maybe they couldn't figure out what to make chicken taste like which is why chicken tastes like everything.

As in the film, where simulation is the reality, *in reality* what we eat today, as I have suggested, can also largely be a simulation. Within our presentday matrix, the interconversion of foods by 'machines'—that is, our own technologies of food, flavour, and image synthesis—makes of food a *substrate:* a base product to which is added not only taste, texture, vitamins, or 'functions', but also added values: *the signs* of convenience, health, or 'sexiness'—*everything our minds need.*

In a deeply ironic way, Lévi-Strauss's dictum that food must be good to think about before it is good to eat reasserts itself at the cutting edge of contemporary taste relations. That 'chicken' can (be the) taste of 'everything else' is but a reminder of how abstracted, statistical and synthesizable 'chicken' has become: battery chickens engineered to industry specifications; the manufacture of various synthetic *chickenized* products; even the adoption of 'chicken' as a signifier—word, image, or artificial taste. Since for most, chicken *means* chicken (if it tastes like 'chicken' then it is chicken), the media-brokered equality between words, *taste* and things remains the undergirding support of our particular 'matrix'. 'Figur[ing] out what to make chicken taste like' is just one aspect of the technical information-gathering needed to produce a growing range of chickenized products.

Both the contemporary synthesizing of taste and the design and production of processed food, appear to be based on an accretive model of knowledge, one perhaps inadvertently satirized in *The Matrix*. Put simply, it is a model long held in contempt and recalls the warning explicit in Mary Shelley's Frankenstein: that (a scientific) understanding of the parts will not allow for a reproduction of the living whole. Such a model certainly sustains the technologies of taste which now thrive with the help of industry and commerce. Treating food as a substrate to which tastes, in this instance, can be added at will, accords with the notion that accretion (or accumulation) is constitutive of knowledge; as such, it lies at the root of the 'knowledge' which produced the microwave oven, the tasteless tomato, and BSE.[6]

What we have witnessed but not thought deeply enough about is how informatic technologies 'instruct' nature. More specifically, perhaps cybernetic control (cybernetics: from the Greek, *kybernetes*, a helmsman) denotes the very form through which we have now come to 'know'. As Paul Virilio puts it in relation to cognition: 'We cannot but notice today the decline of … *analogue* mental process, in favour of instrumental, *digital* procedures …' (Virilio 2000: 2). At the same time, if what we know is what we control, how can this ever be adequately representative of the complex world of organic nature or of tastes, which act as 'messages' passed between organism and environment, those which we have been 'interrupting' for decades? In the *image of control*, taste is yet the corporeal register of a complex communication of living, flavoursome things which have now been overdetermined by semiotic 'cookery' and industrial interconversion.

The flavourless foods of battery production and the processed industrial flavours of the laboratory, mark the absence of real taste. By comparison, living food and flavour and the sense of taste, represent a biologically established nexus of pathways from which such knowledge took form, but which now has been undermined. Given that living food is assimilated by all organisms, including humans, the under-utilization of taste as a corporeal mode of knowing, linked to the gustatory qualities of natural foods, is a serious matter. In part the result of our collective disrespect for traditional knowledge systems, the 'communicational' relation between organism and environment is eroded. One might add that in our favour, as a sense, taste has not lost any of its potential power, but it remains to be seen how interest and overdetermination can coexist.

When Virilio writes of the 'damage caused by the onset of the computerized dissuasion of perceptible reality, which is more and more closely tied to a veritable industrialization of simulation' he relates digitalization to the visual realm (Virilio 1995: 141). 'Our vision is that of montage', he argues elsewhere, 'a montage of temporalities which are the product not only of the powers that be, but of the technologies that organize time' (Virilio 1989: 31). So when we dine out at a local 'Thai' restaurant, eat 'peasant cuisine' at an urban trattoria or consume a McDonald's burger of 'grilled' chicken that has had fake stripes added to the meat subsequent to cooking, are we not also consuming 'hyperreal' foods that occupy a space within a dissuaded reality?[7] Dissuasion may in fact be the new form of *persuasion*: a word derived from the Indo-European word, *swad*, meaning to sweeten and persuade. Yet, whether one is being persuaded by the actual sensual qualities of food or dissuaded within the technosphere, the question must be asked: is the 'space' of sensory experience not always that of a dissuaded reality, in so far as this is always-already one mediated and constituted by a montage of corporeal and cognitive effects—and by substances and signs? The common understanding that the visual-aesthetic appeal of food is directly linked to taste satisfaction appears to affirm a reality (rather than the hyperreality) of the visual-gustatory montage of flavours, signs, and substances.

As mentioned, in *The Matrix* the eponymously named digitalized construct of reality allows humans to 'live, breathe, smell, see, hear, touch, and taste', yet at the same time be no more than immersed digital entities. One scene in particular provides the occasion for an elementary cybernetics lesson on the separation of cognition from sense experience and so puts the question of whether we live in a 'dissuaded reality' or not nicely in perspective.

So that he can better carry out his dangerous mission against 'the machines' inside the matrix, the hero, Neo (played by Keanu Reaves), must first be convinced by his mentor, Morpheus (played by Laurence Fishburne), that what he has previously 'experienced' is not real.

> MORPHEUS: What is 'real'? How do you define 'real'? If you are talking about what you can feel, what you can smell, what you can taste and see then 'real' is simply electrical signals interpreted by your brain.

This logic is based on the cybernetic principle that nothing which happens in the brain is 'real' in the sense that our experience of something 'really happening' is not simultaneously the register of an event occurring in a world 'out there'. The real is always-already the result of cognitive processing. Put another way, sensory experiences are the product of the digital processing of analogue information received from sense receptors.[8] Therefore, the term 'reality' can only ever relate to the already processed information received from the environment, constituting an objective complement of material relations which remains unknown. In this context, 'the result of mental information processing is an artificial reality' whereby 'sensory modes only launch the constmction of this artificial reality, the only reality we can know' (Kampis 1993: 142, 143).

Signs, representations, and 'electrical impulses' appear to be the principal shaping forces of perceivable reality. In relation to food and taste, I would therefore reject the notion that some 'undissuaded reality' is an open possibility; that taste could be deconditioned or, as such, lead us in search of some perfect diet. But gustatory experience in the contemporary world is doubly conditioned: by cognitive processing and by a hyperreal mediation whereby foods, flavours, conceptual understandings, and attitudes are knowingly manipulated. Without engaging with taste *as a mode of knowing* in its own right, means experiencing sensory taste as gustatory effect; as taste sensations cut off from any real knowledge of the morsel which transports them. Taste has the power to create a sensory bridge to a living reality 'outside the matrix', one which implies an ecology of inclusion and relationship between culture and nature; one that promotes the activity of knowing as accessible, engaging and corporeal, rather than one pre-tuned for reception. Sea, sun, air, soil, and water produce food and taste within interconnected living systems in which humans have evolved and often thrived; by our own efforts, we have learned how to enjoy the limits of taste relations. The sensory mode we call taste is surely one 'flavoured' by culturally variable, yet corporeally robust, inter-sense relationships and linked perceptions, as much as by natural and culinary histories, cultural discourses, ideas and beliefs, and by food production and consumption practices. As Neo must learn he is a fake before he can be real, so too as tasters we must also learn how taste is, and has been, constructed before we might benefit from re-engagement with the chains of forces and processes which link taste to a living and organic reality. The cultural 'physiology' of taste is fragile and variable. Consequently, it has been overdetermined by forces like those outlined above. Taste has powers which nature's largesse has provided for our pleasure and as a source of knowledge, but that pleasure and knowledge also depend on whether we actively exercise our 'taste' rather than allow it to be adversely influenced in ways which we have not yet paid enough attention to.

NOTES

1. See Roland Barthes (1979), 'Toward a psychosociology of contemporary food consumption', in Forster and Ranum (eds.), *Food and Drink in History: Selections from the Annales*, Vol 5, Baltimore: Johns Hopkins University Press, a seminal paper dealing in part with the versatile and at times contradictory cultural meaning of 'sweetness'.
2. See Rachel Laudan (2001), 'A plea for culinary modernism: why we should love new, fast, processed food', in *Gastronomica* 1:1, February: 36–44.
3. Of course, the present-day obesity crisis reveals that, particularly in relation to the links between advertising, television, and childhood behaviour patterns, there is evidence enough to support the notion that personal ideals can have little or nothing to do with what people choose to eat. Surely it is more their absence that brings disaster. Notwithstanding, the physical effects of semiological manipulation are also frighteningly apparent. The fact that television-viewing time has been linked to obesity provides us with a physiological explanation for 'fatness', and without even contemplating how the eating-related messages gleaned while watching also contribute to an individual's eating habits.
4. A phrase which echoes that of the Slow Food Movement's 'Ark of Taste'. 'The Ark of Taste aims to rediscover, catalogue, describe, and publicize forgotten flavours. It is a metaphorical recipient of excellent gastronomic products that are threatened by industrial standardization, hygiene laws, the regulations of large-scale distribution and environmental damage', http://www.slowfoodfoundation.com/eng/arca/lista. lasso. Accessed 15 July, 2004.
5. 'The snack food of the future could rely more on sensations in the mouth than flavour or texture. Food companies are experimenting with "sensates" … to make your mouth

tingle, warm, cool, salivate, or tighten … the next step is to manipulate the sensates to change the length or intensity of the sensation'. Caitlin Fitzsimmons, 'Snacks to be a real sensation', *The Australian*, 20 August, 2003.

6. Bovine Spongiform Encephelopathy, or 'mad cow disease', devastated the UK beef trade from the mid-1980s to the mid-90s. It was caused in part by feeding cattle products to cattle. The deadly human equivalent is known as Creutzfeldt-Jacob Disease.

7. In Sydney, Australia, McDonald's ceased production of its 'grilled' McChicken burgers after authorities found McDonald's product-related advertising 'constituted misleading or deceptive conduct'. It was discovered that the 'grill' marks usually associated with barbecue-style cooking over a hot grill were in fact applied—after cooking—by 'a hot roller'. See article, 'Mac chick is plucked', *Sydney Morning Herald*, 18 June, 1999: 3.

8. For an information-theory description of sense-perception, see, Fred I. Dretske, *Knowledge and the Flow of Information*, Stanford: CSLI Publications, 1999 [MIT Press, 1981]: 135ff.

REFERENCES

Barthes, R. (1972), *Mythologies*, St Albans: Paladin.

——. (1979), 'Toward a psychosociology of contemporary food consumption', in R. Forster and O. Ranurn (eds), *Food and Drink in History: Selections From the Annales*, Vol. 5, Baltimore: Johns Hopkins University Press.

Baudrillard, J. (1990), 'The Pseudo-event and neo-reality', in *Revenge of the Crystal: Selected Writings on the Modern Object and its Destiny*, 1968–1983, Sydney: Power Institute/Pluto Press.

Berthelot, M. (1894), 'En 1'an 2000', paper given at the banquet for the Chambre Syndicate des Produits Chimiques.

Borgmann, A. (1984), *Technology and the Character of Everyday Life*, Chicago: Chicago University Press.

Borgstrom, Georg (1969), *Principles of Food Science, Vol. 1: Food Technology*, London: MacMillan.

Camporesi, P. (1998), *The Magic Harvest: Food, Folklore and Society*, trans. J. K. Hall, Cambridge: Polity Press.

Cantor, S. M., and Cantor, M. B. (1967), 'Socioeconomic factors in fat and sugar consumption', in M. Kare and O. Maller (eds), *The Chemical Senses and Nutrition*, New York: Academic Press.

de Certeau, M., Giard L. and Mayol P. (eds) (1998), *The Practice of Everyday Life*, Vol. II, trans. T. J. Tomasik, Minneapolis: University of Minnesota Press.

Dretske, F. (1999), *Knowledge and the Flow of Information*, Stanford: CSLI Publications.

Engel, M. (2001), 'That green vegetable: who needs it?', *Sydney Morning Herald*, 25 February.

Fitzsimmons, C. (2003), 'Snacks to be a real sensation', *The Australian*, 20 August.

Kampis, G. (1993), 'On understanding how the mind is organised: cognitive maps and the "physics" of mental information processing', in Laszlo, Masulli, Artigiani and Csányi (eds), *The Evolution of Cognitive Maps: New Paradigms for the Twenty-First Century*, Amsterdam: Gordon and Breach.

Lauden, Rachel (2001), 'A plea for culinary modernism: why we should love new, fast, processed food', in *Gastronomica* 1 (1): February.

Levenstein, H. (1993), *Paradox of Plenty: A Social History of Eating in America*, New York: Oxford University Press.

Luhmann, N. (2000), *The Reality of the Mass Media*, trans. Kathleen Cross, Cambridge: Polity Press.

Mason, A. (1955), *Cook a Good Dinner with Anne Mason*, Melbourne: Whitcombe and Tombs.

No author cited (1975), *The Amana Guide to Great Cooking with a Microwave Oven*, New York: Popular Library.

Nestlé, M. (c.2002), *Food Politics: How the Food Industry Influences Nutrition and Health*. Berkeley: University of California Press.

Schlosser, Eric (2001), *Fast Food Nation: The Dark Side of the All-American Meal*, New York: Houghton Mifflin.

Scribner, G. (1978), *The Quick and Easy Microwave Oven Cookbook*, New York: Weathervane.

Shephard, S. (2000), *Pickled, Potted and Canned. The Story of Food Preserving*, London: Headline.

Toops, D. (1998), 'Forecasts for the millennium: advertising gurus predict meals on wheels, pizza-flavoured corn', in *Food Processing*, Nov, V. 59.

Virilio, P. (2000), *The Information Bomb*, trans. Chris Turner, London: Verso.

——. (1995), *The Art of the Motor*, trans. J. Rose, Minneapolis: University of Minnesota Press.

——. with Lotringer, S. (1989), *Pure War*, trans. M. Polizotti, New York: Semiotext(e).

THE PLEASURES OF EATING

By Wendell Berry

Many times, after I have finished a lecture on the decline of American farming and rural life, someone in the audience has asked, "What can city people do?"

"Eat responsibly," I have usually answered. Of course, I have tried to explain what I mean by that, but afterwards I have invariably felt there was more to be said than I had been able to say. Now I would like to attempt a better explanation.

I begin with the proposition that eating is an agricultural act. Eating ends the annual drama of the food economy that begins with planting and birth. Most eaters, however, are no longer aware that this is true. They think of food as an agricultural product, perhaps, but they do not think of themselves as participants in agriculture. They think of themselves as "consumers." If they think beyond that, they recognize that they are passive consumers. They buy what they want—or what they have been persuaded to want—within the limits of what they can get. They pay, mostly without protest, what they are charged. And they mostly ignore certain critical questions about the quality and the cost of what they are sold: How fresh is it? How pure or clean is it, how free of dangerous chemicals? How far was it transported, and what did transportation add to the cost? How much did manufacturing or packaging or advertising add to the cost? When the food product has been manufactured or "processed" or "precooked," how has that affected its quality or price or nutritional value?

Most urban shoppers would tell you that food is produced on farms. But most of them do not know what farms, or what kinds of farms, or where the farms are, or what knowledge of skills are involved in farming. They apparently have little doubt that farms will continue to produce, but they do not know how or over what obstacles. For them, then, food is pretty much an abstract idea—something they do not know or imagine—until it appears on the grocery shelf or on the table.

The specialization of production induces specialization of consumption. Patrons of the entertainment industry, for example, entertain themselves less and less and have become more and more passively dependent on commercial suppliers. This is certainly true also of patrons of the food industry, who have tended more and more to be mere consumers—passive, uncritical, and dependent. Indeed, this sort of consumption may be said to be one of the chief goals of industrial production. The food industrialists have by now persuaded millions of consumers to prefer food that is already prepared. They will grow, deliver, and cook your food for you and (just like your mother) beg you to eat it. That they do not yet offer to insert it, prechewed, into our mouth is only because they have found no profitable way to do so. We may rest assured that they would be glad to find such a way. The ideal industrial food consumer would be strapped to a table with a tube running from the food factory directly into his or her stomach.

Perhaps I exaggerate, but not by much. The industrial eater is, in fact, one who does not know that eating is an agricultural act, who no longer knows or imagines the connections between eating and the land, and who is therefore necessarily passive and uncritical—in short, a victim. When food, in the minds of eaters, is no longer associated with farming and with the land, then the eaters are suffering a kind of cultural amnesia that is misleading and dangerous. The current version of the "dream home" of the future involves "effortless" shopping from a list of available goods on a television monitor and heating precooked food by remote control. Of course, this implies and depends on, a perfect ignorance of the history of the food that is consumed. It requires that the citizenry should give up their hereditary and sensible aversion to buying a pig in a poke. It wishes to make the selling of pigs in pokes an honorable and glamorous activity. The dreams in this dream home will perforce know nothing about the kind or quality of this food, or where it came from, or how it was produced and prepared, or what ingredients, additives, and residues it contains—unless, that is, the dreamer undertakes a close and constant study of the food industry, in which case he or she might as well wake up and play an active an responsible part in the economy of food.

There is, then, a politics of food that, like any politics, involves our freedom. We still (sometimes) remember that we cannot be free if our minds and voices are controlled by someone else. But we have neglected to understand that we cannot be free if our food and its sources are controlled by someone else. The condition of the passive consumer of food is not a democratic condition. One reason to eat responsibly is to live free.

But if there is a food politics, there are also a food esthetics and a food ethics, neither of which is dissociated from politics. Like industrial sex, industrial eating has become a degraded, poor, and paltry thing. Our kitchens and other eating places more and more resemble filling stations, as our homes more and more resemble motels. "Life is not very interesting," we seem to have decided. "Let its satisfactions be minimal, perfunctory, and fast." We hurry through our meals to go to work and hurry through our work in order to "recreate" ourselves in the evenings and on weekends and vacations. And then we hurry, with the greatest possible speed and noise and violence, through our recreation—for what? To eat the billionth hamburger at some fast-food joint hellbent on increasing the "quality" of our life? And all this is carried out in a remarkable obliviousness to the causes and effects, the possibilities and the purposes, of the life of the body in this world.

One will find this obliviousness represented in virgin purity in the advertisements of the food industry, in which food wears as much makeup as the actors. If one gained one's whole knowledge of food from these advertisements (as some presumably do), one would not know that the various edibles were ever living creatures, or that they all come from the soil, or that they were produced by work. The passive American consumer, sitting down to a meal of pre-prepared or fast food, confronts a platter covered with inert, anonymous substances that have been processed, dyed, breaded, sauced, gravied, ground, pulped, strained, blended, prettified, and sanitized beyond resemblance to any part of any creature that ever lived. The products of nature and agriculture have been made, to all appearances, the products of industry. Both eater and eaten are thus in exile from biological reality. And the result is a kind of solitude, unprecedented in human experience, in which the eater may think of eating as, first, a purely commercial transaction between him and a supplier and then as a purely appetitive transaction between him and his food.

And this peculiar specialization of the act of eating is, again, of obvious benefit to the food industry, which has good reasons to obscure the connection between food and farming. It would not do for the consumer to know that the hamburger she is eating came from a steer who spent much of his life standing deep in his own excrement in a feedlot, helping to pollute the local streams, or that the calf that yielded the veal cutlet on her plate spent its life in a box in which it did not have room to turn around. And, though her sympathy for the slaw might be less tender, she should not be encouraged to meditate on the hygienic and biological implications of mile-square fields of cabbage, for vegetables grown in huge monocultures are dependent on toxic chemicals—just as animals in close confinements are dependent on antibiotics and other drugs.

The consumer, that is to say, must be kept from discovering that, in the food industry—as in any other industry—the overriding concerns are not quality and health, but volume and price. For decades now the entire industrial food economy, from the large farms and feedlots to the chains of supermarkets and fast-food restaurants has been obsessed with volume. It has relentlessly increased scale in order to increase volume in order (probably) to reduce costs. But as scale increases, diversity declines; as diversity declines, so does health; as health declines, the dependence on drugs and chemicals necessarily increases. As capital replaces labor, it does so by substituting machines, drugs, and chemicals for human workers and for the natural health and fertility of the soil. The food is produced by any means or any shortcuts that will increase profits. And the business of the cosmeticians of advertising is to persuade the consumer that food so produced is good, tasty, healthful, and a guarantee of marital fidelity and long life.

It is possible, then, to be liberated from the husbandry and wifery of the old household food economy. But one can be thus liberated only by entering a trap (unless one sees ignorance and helplessness as the signs of privilege, as many people apparently do). The trap is the ideal of industrialism: a walled city surrounded by valves that let merchandise in but no consciousness out. How does one escape this trap? Only voluntarily, the same way that one went in: by restoring one's consciousness of what is involved in eating; by reclaiming responsibility for one's own part in the food economy. One might begin with the illuminating principle of Sir Albert Howard's, that we should understand "the whole problem of health in soil, plant, animal, and man as one great subject." Eaters, that is, must understand that eating takes place inescapably in the world, that it is inescapably an agricultural act, and how we eat determines, to a considerable extent, how the world is used. This is a simple way of describing a relationship that is inexpressibly complex. To eat responsibly is to understand and enact, so far as we can, this complex relationship. What can one do? Here is a list, probably not definitive:

1. Participate in food production to the extent that you can. If you have a yard or even just a porch box or a pot in a sunny window, grow something to eat in it. Make a little compost of your kitchen scraps and use it for fertilizer. Only by growing some food for yourself can you become acquainted with the beautiful energy cycle that revolves from soil to seed to flower to fruit to food to offal to decay, and around again. You will be fully responsible for any food that you grow for yourself, and you will know all about it. You will appreciate it fully, having known it all its life.

2. Prepare your own food. This means reviving in your own mind and life the arts of kitchen and household. This should enable you to eat more cheaply, and it will give you a measure of "quality control": you will have some reliable knowledge of what has been added to the food you eat.

3. Learn the origins of the food you buy, and buy the food that is produced closest to your home. The idea that every locality should be, as much as possible, the source of its own food makes several kinds of sense. The locally produced food supply is the most secure, freshest, and the easiest for local consumers to know about and to influence.

4. Whenever possible, deal directly with a local farmer, gardener, or orchardist. All the reasons listed for the previous suggestion apply here. In addition, by such dealing you eliminate the whole pack of merchants, transporters, processors, packagers, and advertisers who thrive at the expense of both producers and consumers.

5. Learn, in self-defense, as much as you can of the economy and technology of industrial food production. What is added to the food that is not food, and what do you pay for those additions?

6. Learn what is involved in the best farming and gardening.

7. Learn as much as you can, by direct observation and experience if possible, of the life histories of the food species.

The last suggestion seems particularly important to me. Many people are now as much estranged from the lives of domestic plants and animals (except for flowers and dogs and cats) as they are from the lives of the wild ones. This is regrettable, for these domestic creatures are in diverse ways attractive; there is such pleasure in knowing them. And farming, animal husbandry, horticulture, and gardening, at their best, are complex and comely arts; there is much pleasure in knowing them, too.

It follows that there is great displeasure in knowing about a food economy that degrades and abuses those arts and those plants and animals and the soil from which they come. For anyone who does know something of the modern history of food, eating away from home can be a chore. My own inclination is to eat seafood instead of red meat or poultry when I am traveling. Though I am by no means a vegetarian, I dislike the thought that some animal has been made miserable in order to feed me. If I am going to eat meat, I want it to be from an animal that has lived a pleasant, uncrowded life outdoors, on bountiful pasture, with good water nearby and trees for shade. And I am getting almost as fussy about food plants. I like to eat vegetables and fruits that I know have lived happily and healthily in good soil, not the products of the huge, bechemicaled factory-fields that I have seen, for example, in the Central Valley of California. The industrial farm is said to have been patterned on the factory production line. In practice, it looks more like a concentration camp.

The pleasure of eating should be an extensive pleasure, not that of the mere gourmet. People who know the garden in which their vegetables have grown and know that the garden is healthy and remember the beauty of the growing plants, perhaps in the dewy first light of morning when gardens are at their best. Such a memory involves itself with the food and is one of the pleasures of eating. The knowledge of the good health of the garden relieves and frees and comforts the eater. The same goes for eating meat. The thought of the good pasture and of the calf contentedly grazing flavors the steak. Some, I know, will think of it as bloodthirsty or worse to eat a fellow creature you have known all its life. On the contrary, I think it means that you eat with understanding and with gratitude. A significant part of the pleasure of eating is in one's accurate consciousness of the lives and the world from which food comes. The pleasure of eating, then, may be the best available standard of our health. And this pleasure, I think, is pretty fully available to the urban consumer who will make the necessary effort.

I mentioned earlier the politics, esthetics, and ethics of food. But to speak of the pleasure of eating is to go beyond those categories. Eating with the fullest pleasure—pleasure, that is, that does not depend on ignorance—is perhaps the profoundest enactment of our connection with the world. In this pleasure we experience and celebrate our dependence and our gratitude, for we are living from mystery, from creatures we did not make and powers we cannot comprehend. When I think of the meaning of food, I always remember these lines by the poet William Carlos Williams, which seem to me merely honest:

There is nothing to eat,
seek it where you will,
but the body of the Lord.
The blessed plants
and the sea, yield it
to the imagination intact.

1989